TEACHING HIGH SCHOOL: A NON-FICTION HORROR

Published in the United States by Debonæress™,
an imprint of 31st & Seventh Publishing,
PO Box 290405, Port Orange, FL, 32127.

TEACHING HIGH SCHOOL: A NON-FICTION
HORROR/Dr. Poochie Carter

Includes references.

ISBN-13: 978-0-9904537-6-5

TEACHING HIGH SCHOOL

A

NON-FICTION HORROR

Dr. Poochie Carter

Author of The Dirty Word

If you are:

Employed at Utopia School District
An administrator with crybaby teachers
A teacher with hard-of-hearing administrators
A legislator trying to weed out all the bad seeds in
education
A board member who knows what's best for
   everyone
A parent whose child is perfect
A parent whose child has been emancipated
Thin-skinned
Squeamish
Easily offended
Living in la-la land
In denial
Teaching because you want summers off
A donor/investor
A religious leader
A business owner or school partner
Other...

I welcome you to Elm Street. Come on in!

PREFACE

Teaching, like any other profession, has its rewards. While we are not considered First Responders, teachers are, without a doubt, on the front lines. We hardly make newspaper headlines unless a teacher-predator[1], teacher-pedophile[2], teacher-sex addict[3] or teacher-derelict[4] is exposed. Seldom does anyone paint the lasting picture of a teacher in the trenches. Yes, the trenches. Sometimes, unspeakable violence, parental opposition, political impositions and other unimaginable hindrances overshadow the joy of imparting knowledge and facilitating learning.

I want you to think back just 10 to 20 years ago. Hunger, neglect, abuse, abandonment, juvenile delinquency, teen pregnancy, sniffing glue, student-on-student fights, suspensions, expulsions and truancy were among the barriers to student achievement. Fast forward to 2018 and add to that an increase in the occurrences of suicide, bullying, cyber bullying, student-on-teacher fights, gaming to the point of wasting away, homelessness, electronics addiction and school shootings. As a country, as a community, and as teachers we have our work cut out for us.

Imagine being introduced to 120 sixth graders who hail from a variety of public and private schools, in and out of state. They walk into a new school, a new environment, a new way of doing things, but they bring with them past experiences, beliefs, cultures, ideas, ideals, habits (good and bad), attitudes, pains, memories, secrets, burdens, joys, dreams, hunger pangs, undetected STDs (yes, sixth graders), scars, jokes, aspirations to be top scorer in Fortnite, true stories, made-up stories and audible, piercing silence.

Where am I going with this? Believe me, I didn't know myself when I decided to answer the call of a teacher shortage midway through the school year. After the first few weeks of culture shock—it had been years since my transition from secondary education to post secondary—I decided I'd better keep a journal of sorts, primarily for ventilation and reflection. My journal has evolved into something of a clarion call for all the stakeholders who truly care about the future of our educational system, the future of our children.

Join me on my journey back to my roots: the public school classroom, where I was quickly reminded that teaching is no walk in the park.

Table of (some of the) Contents

October 2017

<u>Nigger by Any Other Name is Still…</u>

"F" Doctor Carter …nigger

Now, I don't know how you would have handled being called out of your name, but I did not respond in the most positive manner when I opened not one, but two workbooks with the same message. Was it intended for me to see? It was left in the room. But then, all of the workbooks remain in the classroom. Perhaps someone lacked the nerve to actually say what "they" (in case this was not the work of one person) wrote. Either way, I was livid. My thoughts went from silence to audible mumblings as I paced to and fro gathering textbooks, workbooks, trash and chalk.

"Are you kidding me? I have been called a nigger before, but at the time, she was a kid and I was a kid. The second time, I could only read her lips as the blonde young woman mouthed the word while bringing her vehicle to a stop in the lane next to mine. Both occurrences were years ago. Many years ago. "Them was fightin' words" when I was a child; I laughed when the blonde did it. But this was different. As a child, I only knew

1

it was mean and I reacted the same way to any name-calling. My laughter at the traffic light was impulsive, as I hadn't experienced it as an adult. Somehow I knew her behavior would have been different had we been standing in a public library or a church or some place without the protective barrier of distance fueling her courage.

Sure, it has only been a few days at this school, but give me a break. Never had a child ever called me that derogatory piece-of-crap word in one of my own classrooms. Not at the private all-girl school. Not in any public school in Fulton, Orange, or this current school district. And certainly not at the nursing school, technology school or any of the three universities where I've taught. I went back to mumbling as I gathered my things like a fed-up wife headed for the door. "Oh, you don't want me here? I come here to make a difference and you have the nerve to disrespect me like this?! Come back tomorrow. Look for me. You won't find me here! Your handwriting is poor. Just poor. *You probably wrote F--- instead of the word because it's too hard to spell."* No, I didn't say the last part, but I was ready to pack my bags and file for divorce. I guess this would have been an annulment.

By morning, I had calmed down and was ready for another day. The ensuing weeks were filled with unexpected trainings and other surprises. One morning I was sitting at my desk preparing for the first period bell when a man walked in with a confused look on his face.

I greeted him as I would anyone else who entered my classroom.
"Good morning."
"Good morning. You are not supposed to be here."
Now, you'd think that was my line, but no, it was his. He was telling *me* that I was not supposed to be in *my* classroom.
"I'm sorry?"
"You have a training."
Baffled does not describe how I felt. I scrambled to open my email for some answers. I didn't see anything about a training scheduled for that morning. I certainly wouldn't have risen so early and driven the 20 minutes to get here if I had known about training. I decided to walk up to the front office. To make a long story short, someone in the front office printed out an email sent to her. In the email, she had been instructed to walk to my classroom and hand-deliver the training schedule to me the day before. She said they hadn't notified her

until late yesterday and she forwarded the message to me. Now I see why the email was really her "walking papers." I'd still like to know how or why the substitute knew more than I did. In case you're wondering, the training began at 9.

November ? 2017

By High School, It's Too Late to Save 'Em

The two (or was it three?) weeks of school this month are a blur. All I remember is an influx of teachers offering their support, welcoming me, telling me they didn't know the school hired someone to replace the substitute, and apologizing if they sounded negative.

Since that's all I have for November, I will share my thoughts on something. Over the years, I have heard education majors, as well as elementary and middle school teachers say they would never consider teaching high school, because by then, students can't be helped. They'd rather have them early while there is still a chance to change them if a change is needed, to teach them on their grade level, etc. They believe that by the time they reach 9th grade, they've either got "it" or they don't. There is some truth to this, but it's not entirely true. Children with discipline problems can learn to behave. Violent kids can learn to use their voices/I Messages. The academically behind can accelerate learning; some can even reach grade level. I have seen it happen. I believe part of the problem is that those who believe it is too late after third grade—you do know that studies galore have shown if a student is not reading at or above grade level by third grade, he or she (usually he) is destined for prison—cannot possibly go against what they believe. In other words, if you have made up your mind that the data is correct, that what you have seen in your own classroom is the final score for the underserved or underrepresented kid, then why would it, how could it, enter your mind that something can be done to help this child? I am of a different mindset when it comes to the "challenging" student. I remember being asked in undergraduate school about my preference in student demographic. I knew even then that I preferred working with the population people are either quick to give up on or aren't' sure how to help. Toward the end of this book, I will share an article that further proves the power a teacher has to direct the path of a child.

12-17-17 DPP

I'm not sure what those letters stand for, or why it's required, but I read somewhere that it looks good to have two of them done by December, so I'm subjecting you to it.

The permanent substitute had given the students a list of vocabulary words. As timing would have it, the vocabulary test was scheduled for the following her departure. I administered her test. The students failed.

On the day the permanent sub handed me the baton, I noticed many students did not write the word or definition from the board. They didn't take anything out of the classroom, no notes, no homework, no textbooks. What are they studying? How are they studying? I asked one student, then another, "Aren't you going to take down the word and definition?"

"I don't take notes. I learn better when I don't take notes."

"It's a sentence. You don't write them down? She was giving you one per day."

"No, I just get a copy of her sheet with all the words and definitions on them." I later met with this student and Mom, who echoed the daughter's position.

"She does better when she doesn't take notes. It's [taking notes] a lot for her."

I could not unfrown my countenance. I persisted.

"Studies show that we retain more information when we go through the motions of writing down some of the information as we learn. It's less than three sentences total: the word, the definition, and the sentence. They receive one per day."

Mom agreed that this was not too much for her daughter and that it would not exacerbate her disability.

I thought there might just be a more effective way to introduce students to new vocabulary than spoon-feeding them one per day. More on that below.

DPP of Two Complete Learning Cycle

Identify the professional learning activity:

Book Study

Identify the topic:

Student-to-Student Interaction

Identify the Danielson component the strategy supports:

3c

Beginning and ending implementation dates:

November 8, 2017 to December 13, 2017

What was the strategy? How was it implemented (over a 4-6 week period)?

The strategy was to incorporate Collaborative Learning during the acquisition of new vocabulary words. I chose to implement this strategy at this juncture after the majority of students across class periods did poorly on their previous vocabulary test using the teacher-led Bellringer approach. In order to increase scores from the previous vocabulary test, the new strategy included assigning each student two words. Students had to find the definition of the words and create an original sentence that required the use of context clues to ascertain its meaning. Over the four-week period, students presented their words to the class during the bell ringer portion of class time and answered any questions other students may have had. The culminating activity was to design a game wherein students were placed in teams and had to work together during a final review of the words prior to the test.

Students on teams preparing for first vocabulary test with teacher-developed vocab game

During the final week, students were engaged in a review using a teacher-created PowerPoint that included student names, words, definitions and student-created sentences on each slide.

What was the impact of the strategy on your practice? How did you know?

Students were required to write a self-reflection essay wherein they offered unsolicited input regarding the new format for vocabulary word delivery and commented on the effectiveness of learning the words more effectively by being personally responsible for them and interacting with their classmates (Fisher, Frey and Hattie measured this strategy an effect size at .42). The vocabulary words were included in the midterm examination and of the four English classes that I teach, all students showed Improvement by either getting a perfect score on the vocabulary section or missing only a few words. Every student showed at least 50% increase toward mastery.

What was your personal learning? What were your next steps?

I have generally utilized Collaborative Learning for group assignments during seat work in order to balance out the load and to encourage socialization and cooperation, but the book reminded me of the many ways that we can use Collaborative Learning and student-to-student interaction for far more purposes. It's allowed me to explore additional ways to help exceptional student education (ESE) and English for speakers of other languages (ESOL) to gain an understanding of more complicated subject matter or in this case difficult to understand or remember vocabulary words. My next steps are to review the curriculum map, my own arsenal of learning materials and design additional opportunities for student-to-student interaction.

Dec 19

To the Passive-Aggressive Student with an "A" Mind and an "F" Grade

So explain to me why it's your junior year, yet neither you, the parent, Administration, nor other teachers have determined that your issue is that you are not being challenged? Have you passed the SSA? If you haven't passed the SSA then what is it that makes you think everything I teach is beneath you? You have the audacity to write, "it's a waste of my time" on a test, but what have you proven? What have you shown? Why are you in my class? Why haven't they determined that you need to be in an advanced class? If you want, I can try to set it up to have you in my ENC 1101 and I can teach you College Composition, but the fact remains, you still have not passed and are clearly in the lowest producing class at the school.

Dec 19

It Matters Who Notices the Difference You Make

Today, with tears in her eyes, Karen walked up to my classroom with a student. She wanted to thank me for not giving up on that student and she wanted to encourage me that despite being given a classroom observation (observations are not viewed in a positive light) after being there 2 months she wanted me to know that I'm making a difference. I have been sick with every cold and flu symptom imaginable, but I have not missed a day. I don't want to lose the momentum. Two months ago I walked into a classroom where students had been influenced by someone who had done a phenomenal job of managing the classroom and providing a safe place for students, but lacked lesson planning and instructional experience. There is a noticeable difference, but it can only be recognized by someone who has witnessed or observed both classroom leaders. Karen had done that.

Dec 19

The Double Standard for Teacher Assistants (TA's)

TA's serve an invaluable purpose in schools. They are students who, for one period out of the day, devote their time to service by being a messenger from office to classroom, from classroom to classroom, from office to library, running whatever errands, delivering whatever messages, packages, notes to students and to teachers alike. These TAs also tend to fall through the cracks, because they can be failing a class while doing a stand-up job as a TA. Apparently, they're also exempt from dress code, as evidenced by one student who walked into my classroom as a TA with at least 10 holes in her jeans. This is a school where dress code is enforced and where my students have missed my class due to being assigned In-school Suspension for the very reason that this student is now exempt.

I recently learned that one of my students is a TA. I said, "I'm surprised that she's a TA. How is that possible when she's failing my class? I suggested that the student be removed from her role as TA and the person to whom I was speaking seemed surprised at such a revelation. Remove a student from

TA who is not passing all classes? Who'da thunk it? I have seen the same thing on college campuses. Students who are actively involved in organizations and programs on campus are also the ones failing a class or two. Since their involvement and role in an out-of-class activity means more to them than academics, it should be used to incentivize achievement. At the very least, each teacher should be able to report effort, or that student is not eligible to participate, let alone represent the school (even if he is your star pupil in Model United Nations).

12-21-17

A Measuring Stick for Classroom Observations

As previously mentioned, I received my first classroom evaluation two months after arrival. Keep in mind I came in mid-year to six classrooms of students who had been exposed only to a substitute teacher with no prior experience in the classroom. My recommendation to any professional who is designated the person to go in and complete an observation is to first ascertain what the classroom environment was like prior to the new teacher's arrival: How were seats arranged? How was information disseminated? How was information displayed around the classroom: on the walls, on the bulletin boards? How was interaction? What were the rules? Were rules followed? Were there consequences? And so on, so that when the new person arrives and then is observed it is not up to the new person to list the changes/improvements that were made.

This educator has rearranged the classroom seating several times depending on the lesson being taught or the activities in which students were planning to engage. Daily standards, learning targets and success criteria were added to the board as a visual reminder for students, as this educator heard through the grapevine that displaying this information was a requirement.

I required students to write self-reflection essays in order to A. be thoughtful about the work that they're doing, be mindful of the progress that they're making, understand the subject-matter connections that we make from day-to-day and how they are to use that information to carry them forward; B. help them to understand what resources are available in the classroom and that I'm not doing anything that I'm doing just to get the exercise. Something else that should be noticeable by any visitor is the Recap Board, which outlines every activity for every day of a prior week. That information stays on the board and each week the new Criterion or the new agenda overlaps the old, but they never come down from the wall.

One thing I noticed about students is they began to make it a point to approach me and ask what they'd missed while absent. They quickly grew accustomed to the board dedicated to "yesterday's gone" or work we completed the day before and the Recap Board, work from the previous week. To the right of the students when they walk through the door is that particular day's date and the work planned for that day. To the immediate right of the students at the entrance is my quote: Yesterday is gone but Knowledge lives on. Beneath that poster is a recap of the work done the prior day for both English 3 and English 4. Strategically placed throughout the room, I have success stories, which are assignments students completed that reflect their effort, knowledge acquisition and talent. Ultimately I will have things that reflect their interests because that is equally as important.

Side note: I sent a reminder notice that my initial request for tech support to connect me to a printer is still in limbo. I have made this problem known to three different administrative individuals, including a former chair, which would make four. Still the information I have across my room is the product of staples.com or handwritten postings in colorful marker.

My Secret

It is unfortunate that I can't share this with any administrator and can't really be sure if it's okay to share it with a colleague, but here's what I'm secretly doing. There's a researcher named Danielson whose work is implemented in schools across the country as a measure of a teacher's effectiveness: is she Basic? Is he Proficient, or can the educator ever aspire to the level of Distinguished? And in order to do so, a certain number of what are called DPP's must be completed in a particular time frame and with approval from God-knows-who. So what I've decided to do is find in these required trainings and mandatory/voluntary book studies and workshops, something that I'm not doing and implement it. The problem is, I'm not finding anything I'm not doing or don't already know. It's sort of like reinventing the wheel and calling it something else. That's what research is a small percentage of the time. So with the book study we read the entire five chapters of *Literacy for Learning* and I chose to pull out something I had just done in my classroom before we reached that chapter in the book, and then for training on Classroom Management, I did the same. You've seen one of my DPP's. It is unfortunate that one's experience and expertise is only viewed to an extent, not requested, not solicited, not asked to do a platform demonstration or engage in a panel discussion. Instead, "here's the required training because you're new to our district. We ass-u-me all attendees will learn something from it, and we will subsequently ask you to prove what you learned and how applied." Whoop-dee-doo.

Dec 27, 2017

He Just Doesn't Talk

There are a few things I do when I want to learn more about a student. I start with the student. I then check records to find a contact number or email for a parent or guardian. If that fails, I contact the guidance office. In the case of this student, I tried all those avenues, only to be told by the guidance counselor the student in question may just need me to pull him aside and talk to him or try his mom at this number. Translation: I can't tell you anything about him.

Exempting a kid from communicating has many potential repercussions. Perhaps this scenario will drive home my point. You don't put a pilot in the cockpit and say, "This is your first time flying. We avoided the simulator because you weren't comfortable there." Or, "We're just going to let this future pilot bypass the simulator because it makes him nervous, because he's not comfortable, because she's not comfortable, but then when it's time to fly we're going to throw you into a 747 and hope you're prepared." That's not how life works and that's not how I teach.

I'm told to pull a student aside and have a conversation with him, because he's really sweet or maybe call his parent because he's really sweet. You (You is used collectively here) have allowed him the last three years in high school and the last four years in middle school and perhaps all of elementary school to not open his mouth when his name is called during attendance, to not be required to participate, to not be required to collaborate, to not be required to engage with other students. You allowed him to earn credit in other ways outside of just writing. Sure, he's passing, but he's not functional socially. That is not okay.

We are allowing students to pull strings and each one of them has his or her own individual strings that they pull: one has gotten to know the folks in the front office; another one has trained everyone to speak for him; another one doesn't even respond when attendance is being taken. She just kind of says it in a whisper because she knows the person sitting next to her is going to say, "She's here," because they feel important when that happens. Okay as long as you feel important in the classroom and that's the only place you're ever going to exist and be and have to live and thrive and survive in this world, then that's hunky-dory; however, that's not reality. Therefore, I'm going to make some changes and it's going to make people uncomfortable. And because the administration, the guidance counselors, all these people that know these students intimately seemed to have been okay with it, it misleads the students into believing this a safe way to exist. The strings are cut today.

Jan 8, 2018

<u>First Day Back</u>

I passed out my syllabus covering the next 5 months. (See Exhibit). I went over it with them and had them sign attesting to having gone over the syllabus and understanding it. I warned each class that communication and collaboration (talking) was required and necessary, that their voices were important to me and I would not accept anything less than their best physical and audible selves.

We then talked about apples and oranges (something I literally prayed about and came up with over the break). I explained to them that each of us has a learning style. I gave a few silly examples of how I learn, including the way I collect information, storing some in my brain and some in my phone, and organizing my thoughts in bubbles before I write. I then told them, "Now you will have a chance to tell me what kind of learner you think you are, an apple or an orange." This got their interest. I read the descriptions of each and allowed them to tell me what they felt they were. Those who raised their hands for apples received an adhesive label (compliments of me and Staples) describing an apple learner and the same for the orange. For those who felt that they toggled between the two, they asked, "What do you think, Ms? Which one am I?" This exercise empowered those who knew right away what piece of fruit best described them. The special moment for me, though, was the exchange the students and I shared when trying to decide which fruit to take. I helped those learners understand why they would lean more toward one than the other and how sometimes the assignment will lend itself to the apple or the orange.

Apples

The Apple symbolizes learners who prefer to have all instructions laid out for them, examples provided and a classroom discussion prior to beginning work. The apple also likes working with a partner or in groups. Finally, the apple strives to learn with and from others and takes responsibility for his or her learning by asking lots of questions for clarification and improvement.

Oranges

Oranges symbolize the learner who prefers to be given the foundational information before starting an assignment. The orange tends to ask seeking and probing questions in order to challenge existing norms or research findings. The orange uses prior experiences to guide future learning. Finally, oranges strive to make sense of the world and people around them through independent learning and occasional collaboration.

The time we spent discussing fruit and learning styles helped to cast aside the stigma of individual struggles with learning (i.e., I alone am having trouble with xyz). Any learner, from the strong to the not-so-strong, can face a moment of learner difficulty. I wanted them to understand having weaknesses is universal. Knowing one's strengths is empowering. Being able to relate to other learners by merely seeing the same fruit affixed to the outside front cover of a folder removed the notion that any one of them was beyond reach.

When we discussed the new requirement to have a 3-prong 2-pocket portfolio folder, I explained the purpose for it; how it shows growth and development from Day One to the last; how colleges and universities use portfolios; and how portfolios are also used in employment to support advancement and promotion. Students who felt they would not be able to go out and get their own folders accepted my offer to pay $0.10 for one of the 25 folders that I picked up during the holidays. Students have already begun working on proper language, positive communication with peers, proper disposal of trash, and cell phone etiquette. My student aide started today!!!

Jan 11, 2018

Smoking Them Out

I had students turn in notes today. I require them to stand at my desk as I grade them and I hand them back with feedback. I do this to smoke out the students who hide. Sadly, too many students now feign working and appearing busy until the bell rings. I have even had to stand at the door, physically block students from exiting and say, "I need your work." Today, I remained at my seat and called students up one at a time. I offered feedback to Zach who never speaks. He had not spoken a word since we met on October 18, and when I pointed out some information was missing from one of his items he commented on what was missing. I said, "Great. Just make sure you add that," and he walked away. Two of his classmates were standing there at my desk and they stared at each other in awe. I looked at them and whispered, "I heard the sound of his voice." One of them commented, I hadn't heard him speak since elementary school on the playground. Another one said, "I remember a time when he just broke out and just started talking to me about, I don't even remember what, and it was a long conversation. Weird, huh?" I said, "No! That's awesome! He chose *you* to talk to!" He said, "Yeah, that was pretty awesome."

If you go back to my syllabus, you'll understand why this was so important. The section regarding attendance and being responsible for your own presence and accountable for your own attendance was meant for him for Bri and for Ciara and a few others. They all talk more now and no one speaks for them. I didn't require it to be hard on the students. I didn't require it because I wanted to make them feel uncomfortable. I made it a requirement because there is life after 11th grade. There is life after high school, and as social as they might be outside of my classroom, I needed them to be social at all times—when it is necessary, when it is required, and sometimes when it isn't necessary, and all the time when they're uncomfortable so that they are not swallowed up by society—to remove the stigma of being different, or quiet, or unsure of themselves, or wanderers who have no voice. Today I heard the sound of his voice.

Jan 12

FOCUS or Guidance Gone Awry

At least that is how the teachers describe FOCUS. Students can't appreciate it. They fail to see the point of spending 35 minutes in a classroom to receive their report cards, fill out a purple form, provide info for a yellow form, watch a PowerPoint video and then start class.

This was my 4th period class. This is also my most resistant group of students. They seem bitter, annoyed, bothered, disappointed, disenchanted, unmotivated, rebellious even. This is the Breakfast Club on steroids. After showing the video, I posed a few questions of my own and we engaged in an honest discussion wherein one individual prefaced his speech by stating he's pretty sure he speaks for the class. No one disagreed. He admitted that they are a generation of entitled young people. "I mean, sure, we are only 16, but we have expectations of our teachers and the teachers aren't meeting those expectations. We're not motivated. I don't understand why we can't choose what we learn. I don't understand why we have to complete assignments that they come up with without our input. The work we're given isn't relevant to anything we're gonna need to know or do in life. We don't understand the benefit of the majority of the assignments that we're given, so what do we do? We choose not to complete them. When he was done it was my turn. Mrs. XYZ was present during this entire FOCUS period.

> Well I want to thank you for sharing that and while I'm sure you don't speak for every single student in the classroom I'm pretty sure you do speak for the majority. And I have to base that on the fact that I see how they light up when you come into the room and they tend to lean towards doing whatever you do if it's chat or watch videos

on your phones or whatever it is, so I know they share those concerns. But let me shed some light on a few things for you about how the system works. There's this thing called the Curriculum Map. Not only does it suggest things that teachers need to teach, but it also tells the teacher what is required content. So many teachers do not feel that they have wiggle room to go outside the box, to bring in things that you would find interesting, and so on. However the other side of that is, as a sixteen-year-old, you might be very knowledgeable about what you are interested in, but you don't have the full scope of what you need to learn. You mentioned that your father owns a business and that he encourages you to finish school, because he didn't finish. The difficulty with that is you see his success without the education, but he had to learn somewhere in order to be good at what he does even if it wasn't in a classroom. So you need to ask yourself what your plan is for learning something so that you can be successful in life the way that he is, if you're not going to follow his advice and finish school. Because for you, it is not a matter of difficulty, it is a matter of resistance. While you believe that teachers don't show much interest or may not take the time to try and put something together that will be exciting, teachers spend a lot of time doing that and as the gentleman in the video said, teachers lose sleep over students.

He interrupted me and asked, "Do you lose sleep, Miss?"

"Yes. As a matter of fact, I was angry just this morning because I woke up at 4 thinking about you guys and I could *not* go back to sleep. It happens, but there is very little time to stand in the classroom and tell you all the things we feel and do in the background, things that teachers go through and face on behalf of students. We have to use that time to teach you and we have to follow the guidelines even if it means facing resistance from the very ones we're here to help." After that, the Breakfast Club understood and believed me. The spokesman, however, was choosey about what assignments he would complete, until his last day. I'm not sure where he went or if he is continuing in school somewhere else.

Jan 12

<u>In Control of Time, Mine and Yours</u>

I attended an IPG training on lesson planning this week. I was also asked to assist an ESE Support person to fill in her pre-observation paperwork. I was familiar with the questions, as I had the opportunity to complete the same form for my own observation in 2017. To find myself completing the forms so that someone else could be observed seemed a bit strange to me. What was even more strange is that the questions on the pre-observation form (and there are many and it takes time to answer them in detail) did not correspond with the lesson planning form developed for the IP guide. I consider this counterproductive and heard many comments during the training of seasoned educators who felt that it was a slap in the face, a waste of time, an insult to the profession, and a few "I'm glad I'm retiring." The bottom line is, there are too many forms, too many requirements, too many meetings, too many trainings for educators who have been in the game for upwards of 10 years. Everything that I've seen thus far has led me to wonder if this shouldn't be taught to the education major, the person who, prior to going into the classroom for an internship, needs to be exposed to this information. It's a bit late and a hindsight approach to present this kind of information to educators who can teach it themselves. And here I sit never once asked to give a presentation, never once asked my professional opinion, never once asked to share my expertise as a university professor or college professor, an author, a college textbook peer reviewer and administrator. After completing the group exercise we hear from the facilitators what a flawed approach it is. So why are we here again?

From: Watley, Jodey B.
Sent: Friday, January 12, 2018 9:06 AM
To: Carter, Poochie
Subject: Impressed to the Tenth Power

Dr. Carter,
I just wanted to give you your props. You handled that situation today in 2nd Period like a champ. That student was using profanity in class that was gut-wrenching disrespectful. Ms. Hayward politely tried to de-escalate him. He became angry at her and started to escalate. You spoke to him and he was trying to escalate again. At that point, he was definitely trying to challenge you in a power struggle. I really thought he was going to explode. But you handled it like a true experienced professor and he had to bow to your power. Wow!

On another note, I was in your class earlier this week and observed that you had to repeatedly remind a student to put away his electronic. I thought that student was going to become difficult and extremely irritated. But you turned that situation around so well that he ended up participating in class by reading aloud(Beowulf), and he enjoyed doing so. Wow and wow again!

Teachers are not told enough just how awesome they are. I just want you to know that what you do in the classroom is absolutely amazing!
#impressedtothetenthpower
Jodey

Jan 13

In Order to do *Your* Job…

The numerous paragraphs I completed for someone else's pre-observation were primarily because she is support personnel and the observation was to take place in my classroom (I left that part out in an earlier entry). There were several items I did not get around to addressing on the form, so I was asked when I'd be able to finish. I had hoped I'd be able to finish it on Friday the 12th but I just was not able to ahead of the things I needed to complete.

When you see some of the questions, perhaps you will understand my irritation: How will the students be assessed? Another question dealt with differentiation. How will I know how someone else plans to use differentiation? It's not so much an issue with completing it, because I know the answers to these questions, but the question becomes, If the person being observed cannot address those questions, why on Earth is a support specialist being observed on the basis of classroom instruction, lesson planning and assessment when they are not responsible for presenting evidence for those aspects of a child's learning? Why hasn't there been an observation form designed specifically for support staff? Something that addresses how they go about enforcing differentiation for the ESE student or the student with a 504 plan; something that evaluates their enforcement of student interaction and/or student engagement; something that assesses their interaction with the students during the learning. Something that encourages them to get more involved in the learning that takes place in the classroom, to get more involved in the lesson, particularly for those students who sit and stare, who are unsure (because of some aspect of their ESE designation) who give up before ever trying (because of some aspect of their 504 designation); something that observes how well they pick up the slack when the teacher is dealing with 18 students while she deals with the remaining seven and sometimes vice versa. This would be an ideal approach to recognizing effective teaching and promoting professional development, particularly in the classrooms I've been assigned.

Jan 17

Why You Entitled Little… (clears throat)

Last week a student admitted that his population or his generation is a generation of entitled young people whom he believed were all his age: 16. I have a message for that generation (Yes, I'm taking his rant out on everybody, but it's really Ramone's fault). I announced that they had one week to secure a specific kind of folder, which at certain stores cost 10 cents, and if they were unable to get their own folders they could freely come up and get one from me for $0.10. I purchased 25 folders, and for a full week, I had fewer than 25 students approach me for a folder until Thursday. I decided I wasn't going to sell any on Friday, if I had any left. I also decided I wasn't going to go and purchase more. I had a student become angry with me on Friday. Yep, you guessed it, a Breakfast Club honorary member.

"You can't expect us to be able to do that, because we have things to do and I got busy."

I retorted, "No one is as busy as I am. No one. I volunteered to do this. No one asked me to. You know why I did it? Because I know some students can't get to the store. Some students don't have the 1.79 to buy a better quality folder, since the ones I required are all sold out. I took the liberty and the time to go and purchase 25 folders in the event someone needed it, but couldn't go and get it for him or herself. Don't talk to me about being busy when you admittedly have no job, and never take home any homework from any teacher at this school. Sit down."

Having shared that, come with me on this imaginary journey to adult life. I'd like to offer this scenario, because none of my students are employed—yet.

You work for a delivery company. The employer announces he has 25 or she has 25 automobiles available for any of her 100 employees who will be delivering for her and are in need of transportation to do the job. "All you have to do is deposit a refundable 25 cents [yes, you read it right] in the coin slot, walk up and reach for a set of keys. This offer is kept open for one week."

At the end of that one week, there are two vehicles left. The following Monday, you complain that you don't have transportation. Frustrated, you storm into your supervisor's office. "How do you expect me to deliver for you when I don't have transportation?"

"I made you the same offer I made everyone else. Not all of my employees have the same needs, so I even had a few vehicles left over. For one week, you sat like a bump on a log and watched 23 other people walk up here and get a free set of keys--with a meager refundable deposit--to a vehicle they didn't have to pay for in order to do the job you were hired to do. You asked me how I expect you to deliver. I don't. You're fired."

1/17/18

Principals Say the Darndest Things (so I've heard)

Met with ESE support personnel to discuss students on her list. She asked me if I had been contacted by the assistant principal in charge of ESE students. She had suggested I be invited to participate in the Department

36

of Education's upcoming visit. I told her I had not been notified or invited. She shared a comment that the principal had made in a public meeting regarding the misbehavior of ESE students who happened to be African-American males, and the term she used to describe them. She said she recommended that they ask me to be on the committee, because she felt that I understood the students and would have quite a bit to contribute to that session. I agreed that this might be the perfect opportunity to call their attention to our approaches and the strides we were making. Also on this day, the seniors prepared speeches on the importance of taking risks, and the juniors began reading Chapter Two of *The Scarlet Letter*.

*By the way, the outcome of the DOE meeting is unknown.

All Students are Our Students...Right?

One of my students from last 9 weeks has a new teacher for Senior English due to a schedule change. We are both covering *Beowulf*, so she came to me for assistance with an assignment to write a modern-day version of the epic poem. We brainstormed during lunch. She stopped in again after school and I realized she had good notes based on our conversations, but she was missing organization. So I looked around the room at the posters on the wall to identify which graphic organizer would suit her train of thought as well as the assignment. We went with the beginning, middle, end graphic organizer and I opened up one of the two dry erase boards I purchased for my students. I drew an image of the beginning, middle, end and filled in parts of those spaces with her notes and then handed her the marker. She talked through the remainder. Finally I helped her to remember to stay in keeping with the epic poet. When she completed her required three stanzas, she showed me a copy of the teacher's rubric, which she said she stole, and we worked together to ensure she achieved every aspect of the requirements including alliteration, metaphor, conflict, characterization, setting, figurative language, etc. This is how my days go. By the way, she informed her new teacher that she was coming to me for help. And what did he do? He stopped in one day to give me a few more materials that further explained the assignment and his requirements. He, like me, did not care where she got the help as long as she was successful.

Oh! The best part: my computer was configured to print to the staff lounge printer. Good day.

Jan 18
Emails Are Thorns

You should have started and/or finished your observations at this point. For your observation notes, be sure to break them up within your form into the 5 components of Anti-bias instruction. Be sure to go back and edit your responses (for grammar and punctuation) or have your mentor teacher review them as well. After you have completed your observations, you just have one more essay to write to reflect on your experience!! You are so close to finishing!

@pcs123Winter2018Cohort_learner

Of all the correspondence I have received regarding training requirements, this one has bothered me the most. It was a reminder of how much course work is required of a beginning teacher. It is one of several courses required atop the certification requirements and the local, on site requirements and the actual in-class requirements. I leaned back in my little desk chair and considered the amount of time it would take me to read over all the materials, communicate with other participants once I found them, visit a classroom where anti-bias instruction was practiced, write an essay, write another essay, I lose track. You see, I attended the initial face-to-face meeting. In that meeting, there were about 12 attendees. Most of them had their district-assigned laptops and were being instructed to log in using the usernames and passwords they were sent. I never received any correspondence, so I was behind. I looked on with a neighbor who was kind enough to share her screen with me. I left there as clueless as I was when I arrived.

Jan 18

Emails Continued

-Tell Me What To Do: I Have Nothing Planned

> Celebrate Literacy week starts on Monday and what a better place to start than our English, ESOL, Reading, World Languages classes. Each day next week a group of teachers will read to their classes and we are starting in

your rooms! Read anything you would like to your classes, Text from your curriculum, a favorite passage from a favorite book, a riddle, some jokes, a favorite poem, a fun children's book, anything you would like to share with them. High school students rarely get read to and they do like it when a teacher does read to them. Make this an enjoyable moment in your classroom talk a little about what you are going to read and maybe why.

We will also be having poem in your pocket day on Monday, ask your students if they brought a favorite poem with them, if they do ask them to read it to you and then read yours to them! Wednesday and Friday are dress-up days, join in the fun.

Thank you so much for sharing Literacy in a different way with your students and hopefully we all enjoy a laugh, a smile, a thought, a special moment together.

Do I need to explain that email? It basically tells me we are in celebration mode for something some folks conjured up, then hand-picked me and my classroom as the ideal place for execution. Okaaaay. Good idea? Maybe. But there's a time and a place for even the best ideas.

Jan 19

Does an ESE kid belong in my classroom?

ESE stands for Exceptional Student Education. I'm guessing, but off the top of my head, I have in all six classes probably 60 ESE students. That's approximately 50% of my student population. As mentioned in a pervious entry, someone from Tallahassee has decided to send a committee to the high school to speak with the people who work directly with those students. That said, I'd like to segue into my day. Kevin Christopher (We'll call him KC) has come a long way from a student who seemed unable to even comprehend my instructions. He seemed to be a student who could only understand my hellos and goodbyes. It pained me to interact with him because I knew there was more to him and I longed to hear him speak, to share something, to express something, because that brief encounter would help me so much in the way of planning my lessons around him. So today was a very special day for me, because he and I had made great strides since my arrival 3 months ago. I called on

42

him and asked him a question. I feel that he was so close to answering. I could see him trying, but other students began to raise their hands, so I said aloud, "One minute. Let's give KC a chance to think about it. After a few moments went by, I asked him if he thought he might have the answer. He said no.

"Okay, let's see if Samantha can help us."

What I decided to start doing with him is pay him constant seat visits. Between readings when students were taking notes, I would walk over to him to make sure he was getting the notes as well. Without that reinforcement, he would not take notes. He would sit with pencil in hand, look around at others, and side-eye me, waiting for clarity. He would be ready but unsure, so I would start by showing him what to write, repeating what to write, and he would get it all down in his agenda. To his agenda, I added, "Answer the six questions for homework." This was actually class work, but I knew he wouldn't be able to complete it independently. I was surprised to see him walk into my classroom during lunch. He opened up his agenda and asked me what I wanted him to do for homework. I had him show me the notes he took today and yesterday. Together we located the notes. I was holding a green pen so it worked out that my bubbles next to select notes would make it easier for him to locate once he got home. I showed him a question and then I pointed to his notes where he could find the answer and I wrote the number next to it. I could see a light bulb come on in his mind and asked him if he understood what he would need to do when he got home. He confirmed and as he was leaving, he turned around and said, "I just wanted to ask you what the homework meant."

Does KC belong in my classroom? Yes and no. He belongs in a classroom where he can get that kind of attention all the time because he'll learn so much more. Sadly, I can't give him that kind of time and attention with every assignment no matter how well I plan it, because I'm dealing with different levels of students and sometimes the assignment does not allow me to have those kinds of one-on-one conversations with him. Why yes? Because in my classroom I'd do this all day if I could. He is one of the (if not the) most hard-working students I have. I have always believed in challenging a student at his or her current level so that they can always see their growth and development.

Many years ago, I worked as a substitute teacher and I was assigned an ESE class (this was before mixed-ability grouping). The instructions I was given were to sit and just keep the students quiet. I looked around the room and saw so many manipulatives of different shapes, colors and sizes, so many opportunities to work with the students. I was a bit peeved that the presence of a substitute would prompt a day of missed instruction. It suggested that the substitute may not be experientially equipped to manage the ESE population. I decided to engage the students. At the end of class, one student told me they never use the items in the classroom. I was not surprised. Appalled, but not surprised.

Our students, ESE or not (this includes gifted students) can do so much more when challenged. Teachers who don't understand that and don't exercise that philosophy have no right to stand before a group of students and call him or herself a teacher.

Jan 21

When *Your* Assignment Becomes *Their* Personal Project

Students wrote their first self-reflection essays for me between October and December of 2017. To prepare them for that assignment I put my definition of self-reflection on the overhead and projected it to the screen. I then gave them a three-part essay assignment with a 200 word-count minimum, something they'd never been accustomed to in any of the classes, that of being given less than 45 minutes to write an essay. It was a major shock and a major adjustment for them, but they have made the adjustment quite nicely. Whether they are planning to go to work after graduation or attend college—even if they're just planning to become certified in a field or learn a trade—or go into the military, they must learn to use their time wisely. Although it's not always about completion, it is certainly always about wise use of time. So on Friday my senior classes had to write self-reflection essays and I absolutely love the feedback I get from them. They reflect honestly, they set goals they don't share with anyone, and they connect what we're doing in the classroom to real life, to other classroom activities and to preparation for the future.

Self-Reflection Essay (Due at the end of the period)

Self-reflection is the process of thoughtfully considering one or more aspects of your life from a critically honest vantage point. Today, you will be asked to think about the work you've done this week in English.

Self-Reflection Essay directions: In an informative essay, summarize the learning you have experienced this past week (January 16 through January 18). Include 1) a summary of the assignments/activities, 2) your personal accomplishments, 3) your knowledge of how to access classroom resources (books, assignment schedule, work missed, graded work, etc.) and how this helps you to be successful. Finally, bring your short essay to a close. Note: In lieu of Item 3, you may discuss methods and techniques you employ in order to be successful. Be sure to offer a starter, use transition words and draw your paper to a definitive close. 200-word minimum

Below I proudly share excerpts from their second self-reflection:

- This weekend I have an audition for modeling and I really needed the confidence to help me this week. In English we had to prepare for a speech about taking risks in life. I'm taking a risk and going to the audition

Saturday. I can either make the cut or not make the cut. I accomplished performing my speech in front of the entire class by myself. English class helped me overcome stage fright. I'm kind of not afraid to speak in front of people anymore.

- This past week was probably my favorite week of the year. We learned the importance of risk-taking and how it can better our personal situations for the rest of our lives. This week was probably the most educational week of the year and probably my favorite week of the year. I feel that it is easier to talk while in a chair, but when all eyes are on you and you have everyone's undivided attention is not so easy One accomplishment is getting up in front of the class and speaking my opinion perfectly (in my mind).

- I came up with how over all this week I feel like I made progress Within Myself and my fear of presenting I also did well on my assignments.

- My personal accomplishments from all of this would be understanding other points of view of risks and how they can help the thing about risks is you hope for the best believing in your gut just because something's of risk doesn't mean do everything because what makes it a risk is the loss.

- This week we read the short epic poem Beowulf. This story was action packed and filled with lots of imagery. To me this was the most interesting short story I read all year. I understood it completely and gave it my undivided attention. The questions after the story had me a little challenged. I was honestly just rushing through it. that's why my answers have flaws in them.

- It's crazy how your knowledge expands without you even noticing it. thanks to the different assignments my teacher dr. Carter assigned I've taken in so much new information. Not only did I take in information but I understood so that it could reflect in my work when I'm writing and when I speak... we've been given many assignments but I'll have to say the speech assignment helped me the most by allowing me to relate with the text.

- Have you ever had a week that felt off? a week that's dreary and barren but productive in a less exciting way? If you understand this feeling or even relate to it you'd understand my week... Beowulf the brave Soldier. Grendel's mother the mighty She Wolf. Grendel the shadow of death, all lines from Beowulf the epic poem. Lines are used in work from this week. The work reflected on your comprehension of the poem asking very important ideas from the piece... I am proud of my ability to overcome my anxiety to perform a speech for a grade. My performance was not the best I can do, but that means there is room for improvement. I can guarantee that the next speech will be better. One of my issues was that instead of making a speech at the podium, I was reading a paper. I will use the resources better next time and learn my material so that I can speak with ease on the subject.

- This week Dr. Carter presented us with a beneficial risk. The risk was doing this speech in front of the class... If we were to do a bad job on this project Dr. Carter could maybe give us a remediation even though she would want us to do our best on the first try. We are only allowed one remediation on a summative every 9 weeks so there should be zero excuses for Dr. Carter.

- My personal accomplishments were probably learning how to properly plan my speeches... I've actually done most of my work this quarter and it's paying off because I'm getting more experience in reading and that's an important skill I need to have... I need to be more proactive in using the resources available to me. It helps me be successful because I don't waste time if I missed something important... In conclusion I like these self-reflection essays.

- ...My note-taking skills have also improved and I can now write notes easier. I also have learned how to interpret text better and use more text evidence...In this time these assignments have helped me become a better writer.

My original reason for saving this student for last was that her handwriting is so difficult to read. It turns out, however, that she was deserving of being saved for last. When I first met her, she was very distant and had a hard time seeking help or showing that she was lost. Rather than turn in work or make an attempt, she would feign writing and sneak out of class at the first sound of the bell refusing to turn in any work. I knew she didn't trust me and feared failure. That was three months ago, but look at her now:

- Our teacher gave us tips on how to answer each question to increase our writing and comprehension skills and also gain knowledge on how to answer the questions next time... graded work helped me enhance my ability to be a better student in English; therefore the errors helped me to have the knowledge of what I'm lacking in and improve upon as a writer. Overall in order to be successful you shouldn't be afraid to learn, perform, ask, etc. Always observe other classmates' work to help you understand, or ask your teacher. It's not a crime. It benefits you. As a result failing is your first attempt at learning. Don't try? Never learn.

Jan 23

Running on Empty

In first period, we engaged in a classroom reading of our text. They followed along reading silently as I read aloud. I looked up to see four students sound asleep, the same four students who are failing. Those are my juniors. I did the usual walking around and touching shoulders to awaken them. Some appeared dead. I am not exaggerating. A touch did nothing to alert them of their whereabouts. Second period (senior class) I had one student that I'd already talked to outside in the hall the week before who was now trying to take a nap. I walked over and spoke to him gently. He took out the book and just stared at it, so I went back over to him and showed him the page and he began to work. A second student who had pulled me out into the hall to tell me he wished to earn an A in my class this nine weeks and wanted to be re-seated now decided to be belligerent while tapping the keys on his cellular device. As I know his life is difficult right now, especially with his mother, I asked him twice if he was going to do any work. He just looked at me. I reached for his cell phone. He handed it over and shrugged his shoulders, so I mimicked his behavior and asked him, "What do you want me to do?" (Translation: Dimitri, I am doing what you and I agreed I should do, and that is work with you. You are not upholding your end of the agreement. So, what do you want me to do right now? Give up on you when you are so close to your diploma? Because I certainly will.) He then began to work and after class walked over to my desk to tell me that he's going through a lot. I reminded him, "You came to me and set a goal and now you're fighting me."

"I'm not fighting you."

"You fight me when you don't do your work." He just stood there as if he had nowhere to go, so I continued to talk as my next class filed in. I said, "I know that you have a lot going on and I know things are tough for you right now, but this has to be the place where you escape and remain focused, because you have to finish. You just have to finish. And if we're in this together, you can't fight me. He lowered his head as if he were resisting the urge to cry.

"Start fresh tomorrow."

He said okay, but he still was not leaving. That's when I realized the need was greater than student-teacher. In his self-reflection essay, he referred to me as a classroom mom. Just hard to give up on students like these. At lunchtime, a student I spoke to first period kept his word and came to see me to discuss his series of zeros, grades that are unlike him. He told me about difficulties with his mother that have persisted since 9th grade. He also shared his frustrations with being in the junior classroom when he was supposed to be a senior and still being listed as a tenth grader; the difficulties with his mother were compounded when she told him he is required to contribute to the bills and he's not even 18.

I got up early in the morning in order to have time to take a trip to the local store to get a folder for a student I had promised a folder and who had also contributed his $0.25. He approached me sixth period and asked for his folder. I told him I got up early and did have a chance to finally get it as promised. He held up his hand to give me a high five. I returned the gesture and handed him his folder. I conducted a data analysis and determined that I have over 40 students who are failing only two weeks into the 9 weeks. During my planning period, I typed up a little note and duplicated it for all 40-plus students. They will get them in a few days.

January 25, 2018

During one of my bouts with insomnia, I decided it was time to place the fate of my students back into their own hands. I presented the competency-based model to introduce the self-paced approach for failing students. I decided to offer (thank God for the idea) varying degrees of support to facilitate a range of learning styles in one setting.

Jan 26

Although this derived from a need to help my failing population, I had each student complete the short form.

Please circle the letter grade you wish to earn in English this year.

A   B   C   _____

(Write your name on the line.)

On Friday, I will provide you a list of all the assignments you will need to complete in order to receive that grade.

I originally typed the letter D as well, but I decided students needed to cease electing the easy way out of hard work and the easy way into promotion.

"What do we do if our option isn't on here?" One kid was looking for the easy way out.

"You write a letter to the front office requesting a new class." His facial expression said it all.

*Kids Say the Darndest Things

- Don't touch my phone (male with felony charges)
- Let go of my phone (female)
- It's just a fucking pencil. You can loan me a pencil for the test. (male)
- Is India in the U.S.? (senior student)
- This pic is in Vermont. Vermont is in the Unites States, right?
- Why do I have to move seats? I'm not moving. (male)
- Can I turn it in tomorrow? I get extra time because of my IEP.
- I'm just using it (my phone) to put on eyeliner.
- Did you hit that? (male referring to a female TA who entered and left)
- You don't wanna see what we look at on our phones. (male)
- It's natural…we don't want blue balls.
- Can I do my black history report on Rue Paul? (Female who came out in February)
- Can I dress up like a male for the Great Gatsby party? (female)

- I'll have to take this up with Kadwell and Fortunato (principal and vice principal, respectively)
- Man, when I woke up, I had three girls in my bed and realized I was late for class. (16 year-old student's essay introduction)
- Can't we just finish it at home?
- Can I go to the bathroom?
- You expect us to write 500 words in 40 minutes?
- Why didn't you grade my paper?
- I know I'm failing. I'll just go to Brain Drain.
- I'll copy someone else's.
- I gave it to you; you lost it.

*Eight of these will be revisited in more detail.

Jan 30

6th period

At the start of class, I had a few students finishing up from 5th period. MW walked in asking about his grades. "Can you add 50 points to my grades to make up for my missing Notes?"

"No I can't do that, but you do have an assignment today That grade will help."

After the tardy bell:

"Class, good afternoon. It's good to see you all again. Listen, we have a lot to do. The three words and sentences on the dry-erase board are your final Sweet Tweets for the list. Once you write them down, I will give you the remaining sentences on the overhead, which means I will have to cover the three on the board in order to pull down the screen. You must finish the sentences in order to receive your assignment for today, so make good use of your time. Take down the three words from the board, then I'll give you the rest on the screen, then you will complete an assignment called Dear Sheila."

"Dr. Carter, how has your day been going?"
"It's been going fine."
"It was fine until sixth period, huh?"
"No, it's been fine and now it's better *because* of sixth period."

[Sometimes I have to go in a corner and give myself a pep talk before sixth period, but I'm not telling *him* that.]

Sixth period is one of my most high-energy classes, second only to my fourth period. The personalities are varied with some quiet, some shy, some helpful and others who have great difficulty remaining in their seats.

They are a social bunch with lots to talk about. The thing is, they each aspire to do so well.

I admit I'd rather they be this way than sad, down, quiet, antisocial and unsure of themselves or their abilities. The uncertainty was there when I arrived, but they are so alert now. It took several of them a few extra minutes to settle down, despite being told there was so much work to get done today.

So, I decided to offer something to overpower the voices in the room. Joseph Boulogne Chevalier de Saint Georges' Violin Concertos did the trick.

"Dr. C, that sounds like *Tom and Jerry*." The class thought his association was hilarious. "For real, you know how they be chasing after each other? That's the music you hear in the background."

His comment reminded me of my Humanities professor who played clips of *The Smurfs* for us to hear the classical music used in the background. It was refreshing to hear my student make that connection.

After a few more comments, I mumbled, "And I thought this would trump conversations during seat work." Suddenly, there was silence. Later, I decided to lower the volume and one student commented, "The music made me write faster."

"Then, I think I'll turn it back up."

I had one dissenter. MW. He sat across the room and did no work, just offered an occasional whisper to the friend sitting next to him.

"MW I'm going to separate you from AL. I had MW move to a desk next to me. He did it with no resistance, but he sat doing no work. I took out a yellow sticky note and wrote: You want 50 points but you're about to get a zero for today's assignment.

He sat up, took out his notebook and began to work. Suddenly, I saw a piece of yellow paper in my peripheral vision. Taking it, I flipped it over to find a response from MW: I need definitions for #s 19-22.

I handed MW my list of words. He completed both assignments today. Before dismissing them, I made an announcement.

"I'm proud of you all. You had a lot of work to do today and worked from start to finish to get it done. And you got it done. Proud of you. Enjoy the rest of your day. See you tomorrow.

One student, Nadier, commented in celebratory fashion, "I have never written so much in one class before. This is the most I've ever written."

I do push the students to do more. There are times when some don't finish by my deadline. They reward me by trying. I reward them with more time. They see that the reward really belongs to them.

1-31-18

I had volunteers assist me in passing back large stacks of papers from the prior 9 weeks just so students could file them away and have them in their new portfolio folders. I had forgotten about the student who levied her version of threats of talking to the leadership when I administered the exam. When her papers were passed back, the zero on her exam prompted a trip to my desk, where she began confronting me with questions. I calmly responded, "Oh yeah, we do need to discuss that, but not publicly." So at the end of class she came over to my desk and just stood there holding her exam. Attached to that exam, I had stapled another identical to the first. We engaged in a discussion, which began to escalate. She argued that the question about the movie was not something she was able to answer because I did not allow them to watch the entire movie. Again, I found myself reminding a student of what *really* happened:

> You're telling me what *my* reason was for stopping the movie. It had nothing to do with an improper statement some student made, but everything to do with the fact that there we were at Day Three of watching the movie--the movie you said you hadn't seen very much of--and I had already discussed with you all each time with pauses midway through the movie, that no talking was permitted. I keep a calendar of the times that I stopped the movie prior to the bell ringing, so I can tell you exactly how much time you had to watch the movie. Besides that, I can also tell you that the question I asked you on the exam could have been answered with a mere 30 minutes of initial viewing. You had far

longer than that. Now the fact that you got all the other questions right tells me what a bright girl you are, and I always look for more of that. However, you have to make a decision about whether you want to write me notes on my exam or simply take the exam, which is the reason I attached another copy in case you chose to focus on taking the exam. If you do, then I'm able to record a grade for you, but if you choose to turn my exam into something for you to express yourself outside the realm of exam content then your grade is already in the book, and it is and will remain a zero.

She took the exam, both copies, went to her desk, copied the correct answers onto the clean exam, left the movie question blank and turned in the updated version. I thanked her and ultimately recorded her B.

In any profession where a person serves as an authority figure, it is paramount that we think quickly and calmly to avoid escalation. When I created the apples and oranges and their accompanying descriptions, I expected her to reject both pieces of fruit. She did not fail me. She chose rutabaga. I don't know how rutabaga would act in a situation like this, but I would have to assume she behaved in true rutabaga form. I have, however, seen a little bit of improvement and some engagement and would like to see that continue. The fact that she chose to complete this exam again without any more contention or resistance speaks volumes for her and I'm very hopeful. By the way, she is the student in my Dec 19 entry.

For the new as well as the seasoned educator, students who are still getting adjusted to or have trust issues with a new arrival must at all times experience a pleasant atmosphere in the classroom, regardless of how they are behaving. I made a conscious decision to only address, not discipline, certain behaviors: eating sunflower seeds and spitting the shells on the floor and desks; leaving candy and gum wrappers on the floor and desks; leaving drinks on the floor; constant moving about the room; pulling the phone out of pockets and hiding it when addressed. Instead, I notified parents, increased the workload, commented often on how I felt trapped on a 3rd grader's playground at recess; moved pretty girls next to unruly boys; and announced the placement of new rules of engagement.

Dr. Carter's Rules of Engagement

1. JL-126 is a Conflict-free Zone
2. Progress before passes
3. Cell phone use only during Cell Searches
4. Your effort determines extra time
5. Make-up work only if absent
6. Homework counts
7. <u>You</u> must track your progress
8. Get missed work b4 school or at lunch
9. Speak one person at a time
10. Respect other people's space/time/feelings
11. No "picnics" in class
12. Stay focused
13. Tardy bell = in seat, ready to work
14. Try, try and try again
15. If you're in your own way, MOVE!
16. **Remember the goals YOU set**
17. Ask for help
18. **Failure is not an option**

These are not the same as classroom rules (with a suggested maximum of three); these are guidelines for interaction and success.

The teacher must be consistent. The temperature must be the same and the teacher is the thermostat. This is the same class where I was asked if that particular period ruined my day. We are three months in. As far as my arrival and getting to know my students, it has been very important that I exercise a great deal of patience, sensitivity, understanding and consistency where my rules and expectations are concerned. They see my organization, they see my standards and they see how high I set the bar. The bar is just within reach and I move it a little higher every chance I get.

Feb 2

The ~~Creative~~ Lying Student

"Dr. Carter, I have a zero in the Scorecard for this assignment, but I did it and you gave it back to me."

Hands me a piece of paper with intricate creases in it, origami style, as if it had been folded for some time.

"I've never seen this before in my life. You have a zero in the Scorecard because you never turned this in." At this point, she stands stunned and silent. She knew she was caught, but mustered a look of confusion.

"I will take it and I will deduct points for it being late, but do not ever bring me a late assignment and tell me you turned it in when you know you walked out that door without finishing it."

"Yes, Ma'am."

The following period:

"Miss! I mean, Dr. Carter, I'ma give you my work today after school. I had to finish this puzzle." I was jealous that my work took a backseat to the same puzzle I had seen circulating around the English building. My teacher instinct kicked in first.

"Your desk is covered in puzzle pieces. I ought to take a blower to it."

Then a second instinct took over. This was a much better distraction than a game on his cell phone, talking, or goofing off. He was committed to finishing. He was determined to conquer this challenge, and he was cognizant of the work due me. So instead of the blower, I said, "Grades are going in before the last bell rings today."

Alarmed, he looked up from his puzzle for the first time. "But you said it's due at the end of the day."

"No, read my board." (Due at the end of the period.)

Classmate chimes in with some positive peer pressure. "Yeah, A, here it is."

A refuses to look up: "I saw it."

Another student chimes in: "Yeah, she grades the work right away; I like that. You always know how you're doing in here."

A: "She's still a Meany." He got his work in to me before the deadline and he finished his puzzle. Typical of A.

Feb. 3 2018

Who Came Up with *This*?

The district offers and requires us to attend faculty-led RIPEs. These are intended to sustain a focus on distinguished performance in teaching the state standards and appropriate assessments. In the first one I attended, I listened to teachers gripe about how insulting the sessions were to the profession and the professional, how they could all teach the content, and how trivial it was to discuss vocabulary for an hour and a half.

In the most recent session that I attended, we looked at essay samples and broke off into groups to discuss different areas of weakness. The group I was in was tasked with identifying ways to help students improve upon **over specific**. The teachers began to discuss this vague term, its use in writing and other terms that would have been more appropriate. I offer you this example: If I'm describing someone who broke into my home and the sketch artist stops me and says, "You're being overly specific," I'm going to ask for a new sketch artist. The last thing substandard writers should have to worry about is offering the reader too many specific details. The example that we were given was an essay replete with quotations, so I suggested to the group that this was not an over specification; rather, this was an over-reliance on the text. If students were taught to paraphrase more and not simply trained to offer quotation marks (because the essay is going to be run through a machine or software that detects the students' use of evidence) then they'd be required to think, apply, synthesize, analyze, not just copy. There is a clear distinction between specificity and over-reliance. We have to know what we are looking for in order to find it. We have to know why our students are doing what they do in order to help them correct it.

In College Composition, over specification occurs most often when students experiment with the Descriptive pattern of development. Professors then walk them through the steps to reduce the number of specific items the student-writer comes up with by deciding which will make for a more effective essay. This is more easily accomplished when the writing process is activated.

A Formula for Writing? No.

Now that I've made the startling discovery that our students are no longer being taught the proper way to write, I must make something very clear to all current and future educators who will at anytime walk students through the process of writing. It is indeed a recursive process. What has become of the beautiful art of writing is that it is now offered to our young peop e in a formulaic sense. There is no formula to writing. 2 + 2 will always = 4. But an introduction + body paragraphs + a conclusion will not necessarily equal a coherent or effective or even a *good* essay.

But a formula has been conjured up: read text, make your argument, cite evidence, conclude. Make sure you have four paragraphs. Once you quote a text (this is what students are taught citing a source is), be sure to explain what the quote means. This lesson is not coming from the teacher. The teacher is instructed to guide students through the steps necessary to succeed on the writing assessment. I have asked who provided this directive to teachers. Teachers' reply: "We don't know." What? Moving on.

Some of my students remember the prewriting stage; most do not. So there is no planning; there is no organization; there is no decision about what information to include and what not to include; there is no thought put into what they're pulling from the text, what they're thinking about the questions that they have. It is a simple matter of "use the sources provided to answer this question." In some instances they're even reminded not to rely heavily on one source. The problem is for one of those prompts they were only provided one source. How does a machine grade that?

Writing as a Process

Dr. Poochie Carter's definition of the Writing Process:

The routine application of written expression (from Pre-writing and Invention to Editing and Proofreading) with an intentional aim toward successive iterations, yielding a polished finished product worthy of the writer's approval and the reader's attention and appreciation.

My college students are a hodgepodge of dual enrolled students who are still in high school, recent high school graduates, a few college dropouts, homemakers and displaced homemakers, retired veterans and others. With that in mind, I take the approach that they're all coming to me with different experiences, from different vantage points and with very different memories of their last English course. Some of those memories are very vague. That is why it is important to begin with the writing process. Once we move from the writing process we then talk about what it means to paraphrase, what it means to summarize. If I'm doing that with my college level composition students, I certainly need to do it with my high school students, some of whom have no recollection of ever being introduced to the concept of paraphrasing. Without ensuring an understanding and grasp of the How, allegations of plagiarism are sure to follow.

2/6/18

I had the students copy and follow the directions from the board: 1. take out the instructions for the Black History Month assignment; 2. discuss what you've accomplished from the list of instructions; 3. discuss things that are still incomplete; and 4. share any challenges you are facing. We walked through those items together and shared concerns and solutions to each challenge. Here are a few responses.

What have you completed?

My first paragraph

First body paragraph-early life

What portions of the BHM assignment still remain to be completed?

I'm missing the 500 words total.

The things that are incomplete are PowerPoint.

Identify any challenges you are facing.

Some things I'm facing are: Not knowing what to write. How to put it together.

Finding a lot of information about the person who created the Lindy Hoppers.

The challenges I am facing are trying not to let my personal problems interfere with the things I have to get done.

There is not a whole lot on Garrett Morgan.

I asked them why they thought we were going over the four items above. Some said to see if we remember. Others said to see if we were on track, and still others said nothing. The assignment helped everyone— even those who had admitted they were shy—to make sure we were all on the same page. It allowed students who never asked questions to become more confident in seeking the help they needed. Even the reason for circulating the room changed from a teacher-initiated check to a student-initiated request for assistance as they continued working on the assignment.

I walked over to my most challenged ESE student, KC, and sat next to him as we discussed the work he had done thus far. He admitted to me last week that he's very shy and that although he wants an A for the semester, the presentation due later in the year was going to be difficult for him. I read over his work and was very pleased to find that he not only read quite a bit of data on his subject, but he also paraphrased every word. At that point, ESE support staff was entering the room, so I asked her to step outside in order to share the KC's progress. She was as excited as I was and stated, "You are doing such good work to bring things out of KC we have never seen." Once inside the classroom, I shared with her what has now been dubbed differentiated instruction. She was amazed and asked me where I came up with the idea.

Ms. S visited during 3rd period to make sure I was able to log into the site for student resources. I was. There are ebooks for students but what I need is audio capabilities for selections I choose.

We had a faculty meeting after school and were asked to bring the State Standards we were planning to address the next day in class. We were also asked to sit with our PLC. I sat with fellow English instructors and listened as one of them related the story of a 20-year veteran teacher who was given Basic on her evaluation, so she chose not to return to the school. As I listened I reflected on my own evaluation and those same measures of non-excellence. If we're not careful, it is very easy to equate time with excellence. I have put in a number of years, but to assume that I am good at what I do because I have seniority or tenure is a mistake. One would expect a teacher to be the best example of a lifelong learner, the person who seeks new and better ways to have a positive impact on students. If the veteran teacher was in fact a proficient or distinguished educator, then she had every right to be offended at such a measure. If however, she was more like the teacher to whom I will introduce you later in this book, then I withhold my sympathy and bid her good riddance. When it becomes about us and not about the kids, we are basic. And with time, we become older, yet still basic.

Deeper into the faculty presentation we were asked to complete what they call an exit ticket and a bell ringer. The bell ringer was first and the exit ticket was to take place at the end, so I leaned over and asked, "What is an exit ticket?"

The teachers at my table were very bothered and offended by this activity, which contradicted everything they said they do in their classrooms: success criteria and learning targets. Success criteria was defined as the how and when we called the presenter over to our table and asked her if it is the same as goals, she said yes. After making her way back to the front of the room she shared with the entire faculty and staff the same response she gave to my team member.

Among the concerns expressed at my table, I believe the most pressing is that when evaluators stop by classrooms, they are now going to look for the alphanumeric standard posted on the board, the success criteria and the learning target put in student-friendly terms, and the fact that many of the students are addressing different standards for the same lesson taught, particularly in English. I listened as each teacher counted the standards and it came to 74. Each was able to show me several standards for one lesson and wondered how they would physically position that number of standards across the room on a daily basis to address everything being covered in the classroom at one given time.

For their exit tickets each wrote a mini paragraph along the side margin of the paper. For my exit ticket I simply wrote of my lack of familiarity with the term Focus standard (which was item number one on the pre-test and since that was item number one I could not move on to items 2 through 10.)

Walking back to the English Department building or one of the English Department buildings, another teacher shared that she would prefer these meetings be spent with having seasoned teachers share what they do in the classroom rather than have someone with no true teaching experience guide us through this process every time we meet. No true teaching experience? What does she know that I don't?

As a side note, in my own records I retain information and record the alphanumeric standard associated with what I do. That is for my own benefit and recordkeeping. What I share with my students is a conversation before we start, and at the end, I explain to them why we do what we do, what the steps mean, why it's important that they follow my steps in order to reach the bigger picture, how it will help them beyond my classroom or beyond that one assignment so that they can articulate that to someone outside of the classroom. If I do a good enough job, they will be able to demonstrate it in use with other assignments and perhaps even in the real world.

One student commented as I was moving from desk to desk, Dr Carter gives us all this complicated work." I replied, and you get it done every single time, don't you?" She smiled never looking up from her work and nodding said, "Yes."

2-9-18

Get Out!

When I reached for her phone, she stood and gripped it with desperate strength. When I felt her second tug on the phone, I let it go. "Get out!" Yanari cried when I told her to leave. Just leave. The entire classroom fell silent as she gathered her things. I had told her, "I will not engage in a physical battle with any student over a cell phone. You have let your phone become more important than yourself, than your education. Get out." I stood at the door and waited for her to comply. I watched as her body language shifted from stiffly defiant to hopeless. Once in the hall, she struggled to hold back tears. "Where should I go, Ms?" I dropped my head, stepped out into the hall with her and let the door close behind me. At that moment, I remembered my presentation at the National Youth At Risk conference earlier this school year in Texas. Where was she going to go? Of course, the discipline office was her pre-established destination, but she had just proved my point. Students who resist being ejected from the classroom are not trying to be in control; they are not trying to get the upper hand on the teacher. Not always. In Yanari's words months later, "I was scared. I didn't want to miss out on what I was supposed to be learning. I belonged there and I felt bad for getting in trouble." Without having access to her line of thinking when we stood together in the hall, I had to operate with what she offered—her genuine tears. "You need to come up with a solution to this. I can't do it for you. You are a senior now and on your way to college soon."

"I could hand you my phone when I first come in the classroom."

"Okay. That will work. Go wash your face and come back."

When she returned, she handed me her phone, and no one said a word.

2-12-18

Sunday, all 24 hours of it, was just a long day, so Monday morning I woke up tired and it was obvious to my students. Some thought I must not be well since I wore sneakers that day. I ran from desk to desk all period, every period until I reached the end of sixth and had to sit down. But I wanted to tell you about first period. I have KC in my first period, and I must share with you my excitement and how well he caught on when we discovered that we couldn't simply copy and paste items from his document to his PowerPoint slides. We had to use control C and control V. I showed him once and that was all it took. You have to know KC to understand why this was so significant. I walked away from his desk to help other students, and every time I returned he had already selected more information from his document to place on his PowerPoint slide. At one point I got so excited that I tapped his shoulder with my fist. KC is Autistic, so he smiled and grabbed his shoulder in surprise. I apologized and we giggled. When we were done working on his slides, I gave him a high five. He made sure to save his information, but know this: he is one of the first students to finish the assignment that is due on the 15th and I'm so proud of him. While his ability to paraphrase is at a fourth grade level, there is no plagiarism. The only thing remaining for him to complete is his Works Cited page.

Feb 13 (<u>This is an imagined event that mirrors reality</u>.)

Rudy asks, "This assignment you are currently working on, where is it on the curriculum map?"

"Well I don't know if it's on the curriculum map. I just know they need it."
"Well we're trying to stick to the curriculum map to make sure the students are getting what they need. Can you show a standard that applies to what you're doing?"

"Yes, I could, but allow me to give you this scenario instead: You're on the road. I'm traveling on the same road, but I'm behind you. When we reach our destination you take off your blinders that have helped you to stay focused on the road and the path ahead of you. In the passenger seat of my Porsche 911 Carrera GTS, you see that I have a friend, a puppy and a bouquet of flowers and you ask me, "Where did you get these?" I tell you, "While we traveled on the same road I didn't wear blinders that kept me so focused that I didn't allow for the additional people and things that might enhance my journey - the additional opportunities that another person might consider distractions - so I met a friend who was stranded; I saw a stray puppy along the way; and the fields to my left and to my right we're covered with flowers so I stopped and I gathered a few. I didn't lose sight of where I was headed. I still reached my destination and I did it with ample time to spare, but along the way I gained a friend I can share my experiences with, a companion that will grow with me, and a bouquet of flowers that I can give away."

This is why many teachers become disenchanted with teaching, exhibiting little to no motivation or creativity. I lose nothing by following the curriculum map, but I lose everything if I follow it so closely that I forget why teaching is a gift, not a prescription.

2-26-18

My thoughts were everywhere today. Please try to keep up. Judy feels there is no equity in teacher pay for English since English must spend more time reading essays (200 to 1500 words each). Students must be re-introduced to the concept of a Starter, also known as a hook. Here is what I tell them: A starter or hook is weak if you are merely asking a question and answering it in the sentence that immediately follows. Have you ever heard of...? Is not a strong hook if your question is an exact reflection of your topic. If you have a quote from the person about whom you are writing, why not use it? If you have a poet or other literary figure, why not use a haiku, 575, or lines from a story? If you have a scientist or inventor, why not produce images for your reader? If your person lived during and impacted the Harlem Renaissance, why not research what that is to increase your knowledge; then share that knowledge with your audience? I'm trying to release a freedom of inquiry.

2-27-2018

Know Your Student & Missed Opportunities

In our PLC meeting (don't ask me what that stands for) the teachers were venting about a number of things such as Turf Tuesday and the fact that we're having students in there for almost 2 hours while other students are testing. The main issue that I have is with a comment made in the meeting. I am concerned about one teacher's missed opportunity with an uncomfortable minority who expressed concern to his mother that he didn't want to study *Huckleberry Finn*. The N word made him uncomfortable. I don't know how he avoids the blatant logorrheaic use of the word across the school campus all day, every day. It has dropped to nothing (in my classroom) since my arrival, but not before then, so how did he cope with the real-life expression used by so many Hispanics and Blacks. It seems to me that would have overpowered the advent of the word in a text. The missed opportunity, as I see it, is the teacher's ability to guide a discussion about why it is so important to reject its use by rappers, some so-called spiritual leaders, and classmates alike. Nothing can make that word a colloquialism, a term of endearment. Nothing. The student was afforded an alternative reading assignment. What's he gonna do in college? To use the words of Jonathan Kozol, "It is a questionable concession."

2-28-18

You've been taught to count words/paragraphs; then when you reach the count you think you've achieved something.

What have you said? How well did you say it? Students were taught to quote and follow it with "this means"... Really? We have to do better, no matter what the assessments are measuring.

Mar 1 2018   *The Great Debaters* (a movie)

We watched this movie as a way to revisit the Argumentation pattern of development. They had already been introduced to Toulmin Logic (not by name, but they were familiar with that style of argument). I briefly covered Rogerian Argument to give them an option when they engaged in their own debates. The questions I asked after the movie are below:

1. Is the young man who played James Farmer, Jr. related to the man who played James Farmer, Sr.?
2. Henry David Thoreau was mentioned by both the Wiley College team and the Harvard team. Who was he and why was he mentioned as part of the debate?
3. What debate team defeated the Wiley college team, thereby breaking their 10-year winning streak?
4 When James had his first opportunity to debate, he was unsuccessful, causing Wiley College to lose its first debate of the year.

What, in your collective opinion, contributed to his inability to debate?

5. James Farmer, Jr. defined civil disobedience. What does it mean? Take a vote in your group and decide if you believe civil disobedience is necessary in our society. Explain your answer.

6. How did Professor Tolson know Wiley College won the debate against Harvard?

7. What is a tenant farmer?

8. Consider one of the debates they competed in. How did they prepare? What were their strengths? Did you note any flaws in their strategy?

Mar 5

The last bell of the day just rang and I was inputting grades to try and be out of here within the next 15 minutes. As usual there's a knock at my door. What is unusual about it is the student who was at the door.

 walked in and asked, (this is the same one, mind you, who presented a folded, crinkly, creased paper) is there any extra work I can do? I went over to Scorecard and saw that she hadn't done the summary assessment, which is one of the quickest assessments I've designed. It is oral, and I took students out into the hall to complete it to determine their full knowledge of MLA formatting. I

asked her a series of questions, the same questions I asked the other students. She answered them successfully, watched me input a grade of 100, and said, "That's it?"
"Yes."
"Thaaaaaaankyoooouuuu Dr Carter!" as she proceeded to hug me.
"That's what everyone else had to do. That's all you were missing. It brought her grade up to a C.

This is a prime example of not knowing what the outcome will be but the importance of simply approaching the teacher and showing interest in your grade, interest in your success and willingness to do or go the extra mile. Peers, encourage your classmates to approach their teachers and take ownership over their success. Parents, do the same. It empowers your children in ways you can't imagine.

I received an email from one of my ESE students who prefers not to rely on that designation or the accommodations offered. Her email: My mom wants to know why I have a C in your class. I included her email address and phone number so you can contact her.

I emailed mom a short note and called. She answered and I shared updates with her:

Tavy has a C because she continues to hold on to an assignment I saw her working on. She refuses to turn it in, so I input a zero for it, as I can't wait any longer. Also, I sent you an email with the same information. I also asked that you please encourage her to approach me on her own. I understand she wants to attend college and later the military. I am more interested in an email from her saying *she* wants to know why her grade dropped than I am to know of a parent's interest. I even move a little quicker. I don't want her to ever feel like she can't approach another human being for any reason, especially when her grades, or salary or rank are at stake. Mom was in total agreement. Tavy approached me the next day and subsequent days when she felt the need.

3-7-18

It's Been Three Weeks and You Still Don't Have 50 Cents?

It is a new month and students are still trying to print out papers that were due February 15.

Since I am new, I don't understand all the reasons behind decisions:
Charging students 10 cents or more per page to print in the Media Center; Offering only the Media Center as a place to print; Closing the Media Center to students during class, during testing, during emergency drills, during emergencies in general; turning students away who do not have the money to print (I have watched students collect nickels to have enough to pay for printing).

I have come to learn a few things about my students and the student body as a whole: most are not interested in wasting paper by printing non-academic material, so printer abuse can't be the issue.

Limiting prints to before-school, lunchtime, and after school makes sense if the student makes it here before school (many are chronically late); if they are not somewhere else making up work; if they don't ride the bus and can remain after the last bell.

I began to ask myself, Why am I requiring them to submit work in class, in person? There seems to be no cooperative effort to ensure timely submission of assignments. I considered having them email work to me.

There is no way to reply to them or offer electronic feedback. What have we done?

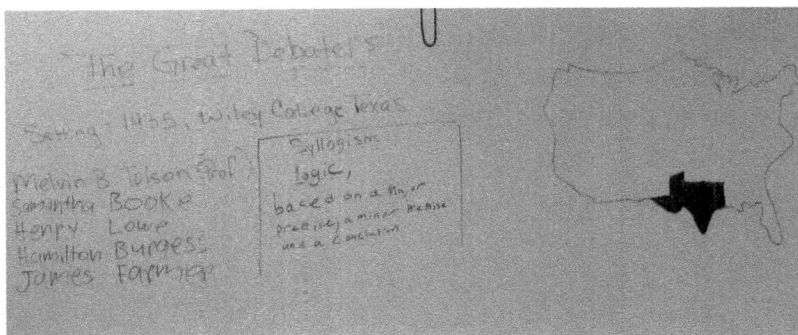

3-13-18

Above is an image of my dry-erase board. On it, I tried my hand at a bit of amateur art to set the stage for the film we were going to watch (Denzel Washington in *The Great Debaters*). A student volunteered to complete the remainder of the board. Prior to my arrival, students had already been introduced to the Argumentation pattern of development and had taken a writing assessment. This is an example of a unit teachers were instructed to begin with early in the school year, a directive handed down from the Wizard of Oz. Teachers objected, arguing that this required a higher-order level of thinking than say, Narration.

After reviewing their scores, I decided we would revisit Argumentation after showing the film, discussing terms used and modeling techniques after those of the student-characters in preparation for their own debates.

3-21-18

IEP's, ESE, ESOL, 504 Plans and, oh yeah, the teacher

The ESE Coordinator for the school is also a Vice Principal.

She presented during a segment of our faculty professional development. I was pleased to find that her content dealt with roles and responsibilities but wondered why it was coming so late in the year. She went into great depth about accommodations and opened the floor for any questions about specific accommodations (e.g., what does more time on tests means?). The Q and A soon became a heightened discussion about why teachers are expected to do xyz and "No, the ESE staff do not give students the answers." Nothing I heard was new to me, with the exception of discovering teachers have the freedom to suggest an accommodation be removed from a student's IEP. The checklist was sectioned off in columns, one for ESE support personnel and one for teachers. There were at least 60 accommodations and numerous check marks next to the support personnel (SP). I have mentioned in a previous entry that I don't see much in the way of support for the ESE students when visited by these professionals. This checklist astounded me, because it confirmed what I had assumed: there is so much more support facilitators could and should do to help students produce in the classroom. My SP are a sheer joy to have around and interact well with my students, but beyond offering a broader discussion of the assignment to those (ESE and ron-ESE alike) already engaged, my unmotivated or disconnected students often remain so. Their approach could be the result of conditioning. Many teachers prefer limited interaction from support personnel. I welcome it.

IEP – Individualized Education Plan

ESE – Exceptional Student Education (can also mean gifted populations, but never used to refer to them)

ESOL – English for (formerly "to") Speakers of Other Languages

504 – A type of accommodation to allow students alternative opportunities for learning the same material as their peers

Teacher –The person who is required to have certification in his or her subject area (math, science, reading, etc.), and ESOL, hours of training in ESE, general familiarity with IEPs and 504 Plans and specific awareness of their students' IEP and 504 documents.

3-21-18

Emails, they keep a'coming

From: Bartholomew, Alyson F.
Sent: Tuesday, March 20, 2018 1:37:55 PM
To: Carter, Poochie
Subject: ESOL

Poochie,
I see you have registered for all 5 ESOL Endorsement courses. Since you cannot complete all 5 courses this school-year, please let me know which ONE course you would like to try and complete by June 30. After you complete one course, then you can register for another. I would hate for you to start work in a course this year and then lose your work if you are not able to complete it

by June 30.

From: Carter, Poochie
Sent: Wednesday, March 21, 2018 7:46 AM
To: Bartholomew, Alyson F.
abartholomew@vasschools.edu>
Subject: Re: ESOL

Good morning, Alyson.

Thanks for letting me know. Since I'm wait-listed for all five, I guess the best thing for me to do is wait or allow you to place me based on which course opens up.

Let me know what you suggest.

Thanks again!

From: Bartholomew, Alyson F.
Sent: Wednesday, March 21, 2018 8:01 AM
To: Carter, Poochie
Subject: RE: ESOL

All courses are open – wait list is our way to check and make sure teachers are signing up for the correct course and also not signing up for too many at one time. We want you to be able to complete a course during the school-year. I will start you with the ESOL Methods course.

Alyson Bartholomew, Office Manager
Professionalism & School Improvement
Winfrey Center, Sandybeach/Extension
2055
http://myvasschools.edu/professional-learning
Home - Professional Learning &
 Schoolmyvasschools.org
High-quality professional learning begins
with a structured planning process.

This process wasted quite a bit of my time when a description of courses and an explanation cautioning teachers that one course takes x number of days would have been sufficient.

A wait list that is only set up to control teachers who might otherwise sign up for the "wrong" course is an insult to the intelligence of teachers. Period.

3-22-18

This entry is about a program offered by the district that I happened to stumble upon

seven months into a nine-month school year.
First, I have to tell you about my lunch.

I brought lunch today. All I had to do was
leave the classroom and heat it up. As has
become the norm, students (seniors who are
released five minutes prior to the lunch
release bell) entered my room, lunch in hand
and made themselves comfortable. I decided
to accommodate students the first half of
lunch and dismiss them the second half in
order to enjoy a few quiet minutes and a
quick meal.
J walked in with his lunch and greeted the
already-seated 5 others.
J is a junior.

He needed to complete a 2-minute
Scavenger Hunt using his cell phone to
access the Internet. "Did you bring your
phone?"
"Yes"
Okay, here's what you need to do." I
explained the process to him, he nodded
and went to his seat. His first order of
business, eat his lunch.
I watched while interacting with the other
students and a few colleagues via email. "J,
you working on the SH?"
"Yes, I'm getting it done now."

Imagine my surprise when I walked over to him to find that he had enjoyed his lunch in its entirety but had no work for me.

"What happened J? You told me you were working on it."

"I was eating my lunch."

"I missed my lunch waiting for you. You don't even have your phone on the same desk. It's all the way over there."

"I was numbering my paper."

"For 30 minutes?"

Okay, sigh, here it is 7th period, my planning period and I can finally have lunch. I choose the unlikeliest of places, the teachers' lounge. It's quiet and something I need is waiting for me on the printer. While in there, I snoop around for novels I can use and find forms tucked away in a cubby. What on earth is a Classroom Supply Assistance Program, and why wasn't I informed such a program exists, at least prior to spending my own money on school supplies? When I first arrived, I asked several people how to go about acquiring these supplies for my classroom. I was given names of people at the school who "should be able to help. He's really good at that stuff." What stuff? Send me a link to this site, allow me to choose the store with whom we have partnered, fill out a form and get reimbursed for my purchases.

You've all done it Or are you still spending your own money? Instead, the document I just found online warns of a March 1 deadline to submit receipts. No need to glance at the calendar on this one. Sigh again.

3-23-2018

Rage, rage against the dying of the light.

I was telling my students about transference (not in the therapeutic sense). I didn't use the word but I shared with them that I rewound a commercial in order to record and share it with them. I was excited to see an advertisement for a medical research organization that used lines from Dylan Thomas's poem to deliver their message of hope and a cure. To the students, I said you never know when what you learn in a classroom will carry over into your everyday lives, because you don't know where your chosen paths will ultimately take you. I suggested that the person who developed this marketing strategy probably got a promotion for creating what would become a powerful marketing tool.

3-23-18

I was reminded today that the English classrooms serve a dual purpose—which apparently is extremely critical to the operation of the school—and that is post office. Mail is dropped off in the English classrooms, the English teachers are asked to deposit, deliver, distribute. Today I was approached in the middle of class by a lower administrator and told that she forgot to deliver a piece of mail to a student during my 4th period. It was now fifth. Instead of taking it to his 5th period class, she asked me to hold onto it until Monday and wait until, not first, not second, not third, but fourth period to deliver it to the student. Note the tone of this next question: but how much sense does it make to leave your office and walk over to my building to hand me a piece of mail to give to somebody you probably walked past in his 5th period class in a building in closer proximity to your own office? I didn't say that to her. I'm sure she meant well. I am just always mindful of time. As a mother and businesswoman, I place far too much value on time to ignore the absence of logic in her reasoning. It could be that she really enjoys visiting my classroom. She does contribute a course-related comment or two each time she enters. Ho-hum.

3-23-18
Us vs Them

I heard several different reports, not just today, but also on Wednesday from faculty members who have clearly painted an Us Versus Them picture on the canvas of academia. Parents are upset with teachers; teachers don't feel supported by Administration; Administration is concerned about the way the school is viewed by the district and by the board and ultimately I guess by the Department of Education, because admonitions and reminders are always accompanied by "This will reflect on your evaluation." I have seen teachers who in the spiritual realm have their hair standing on end for fear of a negative evaluation or a less-than-superb or exemplary reflection of their professionalism and performance and then somewhere in the mix is Student Success. If you find it let me know.

3-24-18

Does Anybody Know What Students Really Need?

In our RIPES meetings, whether they are district-wide or on-site, every presenter models what they expect the teachers to be doing in their own classrooms. In class, we start with a bell ringer, which is a five- minute or less activity that all students participate in. After the bell ringer the presenter will use the projector to show us our learning targets. In the classroom, we are to use our learning targets to align State Standards to instruction, and we go over this every single week in our RIPES meetings. It is evident that administrators are striving to instill this so that it becomes automatic and as regulated as breathing.

I am not a resister. I'm not rebellious, but I am a seasoned educator and as such, I still use what I have always called mini lessons. I've called them mini lessons since 1989 when I first set foot into a classroom a few counties over. The mini lessons were always designed not just to get students in their seats and quiet, but also to review critical skills or information. The other thing that we are now required to do is post the actual alphanumeric standard, "I" statements for students, vocabulary, and a number of other things throughout the classroom.

On some Fridays I require my students to write self-reflection essays. I have it on the screen for their review. Beneath the term's definition, I specifically identify the time that I want them to reflect on. It is always the previous Monday through Thursday unless I want them to cover the prior two weeks. Occasionally I will remind them of the reason that I have them write self-reflection essays. But on Friday, March 23, I paused after allowing them time to read the definition and the instructions and I asked them, "Why do you think I have you write self-reflection essays?" And every class had the right answer. I took it a step further and I pulled up the curriculum map for the State's 11th and 12th graders, which includes all the standards for language arts. A student who voluntarily stood at the screen as if channeling Vanna White, began to point and move his hand wherever I directed him as I explained to them what the alphanumeric portion of the standards were, what the explanations were, that each class, grade and subject is required to be familiar with not only the standard but how to align those standards with subject matter and assignments and assessments. To explain the term standard, I held my right hand above my head and said, "If I were to set the standard here, what that means to you is if you're operating or performing below this mark, it is my responsibility to prepare lesson plans that will engage you and move you up in your skills and your knowledge to either reach that standard or exceed that standard." I then pointed to the side of my classroom where I have an entire wall dedicated to learning targets. My student walked over to that area, again voluntarily, and began pointing at my laminated posters. I asked my students, "How many of you, either in my class or in a different class, know what's on the walls in those classrooms?"

"We don't look at the walls; we don't know what's on the walls in our other classrooms."

I asked, "Did you know what was on those laminated posters?"

"No, We know what's on the Recap Board and the board that tells us what we missed if we were absent, and what we're doing today on that other board."

"Okay thanks for being honest. Now let me tell you the reason I asked these questions. Our state requires that teachers do certain things because they want to make sure you get everything you need out of this educational experience. If we had a guest in our classroom, they would look for the things we just talked about. If they were to ask you about learning targets or standards you may not be in tune with those terms, but if you were asked what are you learning in Dr. Carter's classroom, you would say exactly what you say in your self-reflection essays."

We learn for language, we learn for effective communication, we learn for critical and creative thought, we learn for life. I want my students to understand the day-to-day steps we take to reach their individual and our collective targets. Self-directed learning is stressed when students become college students, but there is only a very small gap of transition time between high school and college. Self-directed learning and student-centered learning should work in tandem and as early as students show signs of readiness to ensure optimal success.

3-26-18

I had my second unannounced observation in less than a week (one teacher told me during lunch he had not been observed all school year) as he formed a zero with his fingers. Well, I'm new. A new-hire needs a bit more attention in order to ensure a good fit. Still, I wish the observations did not seem forced/rushed.

As I was completing the required self-assessment and other paperwork for tomorrow's post-observation appointment, I heard another teacher say she thinks it's ridiculous to complete a self assessment wherein the teacher rates him or herself only to have the "observer" tell you her rating is different and then you engage in discussions to determine which scores, yours or hers, will go in as your final assessment. I can easily surmise this approach was adopted as a way to resolve the previous method whereby the teacher had no room for input. It is difficult to strike a balance.

Last week's workshop presenter lauded Danielson's research before starting his presentation. One teacher in the lounge today sarcastically mimicked him: "Yeah and since everybody in the nation is using her method, it must be right."

3-28-18

Matthias Mitchell and Adonijah Davis quietly observed the following as it unfolded in my classroom during lunch:

Student came by to inquire about Brain Drain work. I told her I was just returning after being out yesterday and once I got caught up with today's and yesterday's assignments, I'd be able to get to the assignments for Brain Drain. She did not like that answer.

"You're gonna be the reason I don't graduate."

"*You're* going to be the reason you don't graduate."

"You didn't give me the work I needed from the last quarter. You only gave me two assignments out of ten."

"Did you complete those two?"

"You only gave me two."

"You need to be in class in order to get the work.

"That's what lunch is for."

"I have an entire 2nd period dedicated to you. You need to be in attendance. Are your absences excused?"

"I don't know. I think so. They should be."

"Okay, the first thing you should do is complete the assignments you've been given. You're running out of time."

"You're a great teacher."

"Goodbye."

Talked to MB after this and he confirmed that all is a go for his departure from the school and district. He said, "No teacher gets distinguished (D) or even proficient (P) because there is a cap on the number of D and P you can get. So Basic pretty much runs free."

"If that's true, then they need basic teachers working here."

3-28-18

Is There a Lifeguard on Duty?

I just spent my planning period creating documents and going through old records to satisfy the requirement of brain drain. Translation, Brain Drain is for slackers who don't even show up for class and who would make the school look bad if the numbers are low because too many seniors have decided to sleep in.

As I scroll through emails looking at all the different make-up dates and Excel spreadsheets for all these students to make up assessments and make up tests and retake this and retake that, it just confirms the fact that this school and probably many of the schools just like it are designed and set up to spend more time and require more of a teacher to remediate or to improve the numbers or the statistics than they are concerned about teaching. Granted, administration really does want teaching and learning to be taking place, but the approach is out of whack. These kids are not prepared. My students are more prepared than they were when I got here, but they are nowhere near where they should or could be. I'm a better teacher than I am a swimmer, but I spend more time swimming through paperwork. I'm gonna need a lifeguard, a life jacket, or a lifeline in a minute.

Brain Drain is an Alias, but stay with me.

I borrowed another teacher's contract for Brain Drain. There are requirements and there are exemptions for Brain Drain. To meet eligibility requirements, students must have earned at least a 49% for the quarter. I've shared with you the importance of time. Brain Drain contracts take up a great deal of time. Many students never show up to retrieve contracts in order to begin work. Brain Drain. That's quite a term. It's a strong term intended to have strong connotative power, but it is extremely weak in practice. Remember the student who was prepared to blame me if she didn't graduate? Well she is among many who are exempt from the 49% threshold. Because she is a senior, her 0% average is not a disqualifier.

Between preparing six of those documents, grading process essays, scavenger hunts, anticipation guides and other papers, preparing for the tutoring sessions that go on each Monday and Tuesday, and evacuating my home due to a 104-acre fire, I could not find the time or energy to complete the required self-assessment for a post-conference of an unannounced classroom evaluation. My plate runneth over.

Side note: I must dedicate an entry to the teachers. I will do my very best to help parents and non-teachers all over the world, politicians and any other decision-maker understand why this thing you call a salary is really just a tip.

3-30-18

All I could see was his happy, jovial, carefree face, and all I could imagine was how quickly he says whatever he wants to say to whomever. It could be an authority figure, it has been me, and it's definitely constantly his peers. I didn't ask why it happened. I didn't ask for any details, but it led me to my previous concerns for the fact that parents and educators alike, including Administration, have somehow dropped the ball on mandating accountability from our kids. As they age, they must be handed the mantle of responsibility and maturity and if they're not, if that mantle is not replaced on a regular basis with a heavier burden of responsibility and maturity, they end up being silly and having very little, if any, self control or discipline. He is a junior. Sadly, I see it in too many of my seniors. It takes me back to the students who were never required to speak in class, not even to answer to their names during roll call. All of them do now respond and even participate in class, except for one. The one that I recommended for honors. I regret the recommendation partly because I'm not sure if he'll be able to handle it, partly because of what I saw in class today. When I called his name several times to report the source he had been working on, he retreated. All students were called on, all students responded. He made eye contact with me several times as if he had hoped this scene would go away. He speaks to me, but only in close proximity. It is a milestone but not nearly enough.

3-31-18

Peer Pressure, Vengeance or Unmitigated Gall?

On March 30, a student in my sixth period class was reportedly jumped by a group of students in his 5th period class. My students were advising me of why he was not in attendance. According to them, his fifth period teacher answered a knock at her door to let a group of boys in who obviously did not have a pass. They commenced assaulting him right there in the classroom and between 10 and 17 administrators (again, according to the students) had to come in and break it up. Who pulls together a gang of friends to enter a classroom, during class, to assault another kid? Who has those kinds of b***s? I guess students choose their battles. They also choose their classrooms.

April 2

In Case You're Interested

Teachers sign in, check their boxes, go to their classrooms, turn on their laptops, log on to the school's portal, set up the bell ringer, set up the announcements, organize paperwork, prepare to pass back graded work and anything else they can do within the few minutes before the first bell rings. When the tardy bell rings, everybody stands for the pledge and then they listen to announcements. Then the teacher has to play a second set of announcements on YouTube. Classes are scheduled back-to-back and teachers are required to set aside a portion of their lunchtime as office hours. Brain Drain requires additional time. Time to prepare the assignments and revisit the work from a previous quarter. Time to grade this work atop current work that requires grading. There's more in case you're interested.

There's always more, but you'd have to follow us home. If you want to imagine a day in the life of an ESE teacher, you couldn't follow them at all, unless you were in really good shape.

April 5

I left early (15 minutes before the bell to be exact) just to be honest about my time off. I was sick. Coughing and chest pain.

I notified my chair via email.
Did you let Mr. Z know? Did you arrange for coverage? Feel better!

No I didn't let him know but I will now. (In my mind I'm thinking, "Let him know for what?" Is this not an email you can forward to him as the chair? Coverage? I have planning.)

4-17-18

A Responsible Student

I received this email from Gavin: Srry that I haven't been there mostly all week hopefully I can still do that the part 1 and part 2 of that test tomorrow my family been looking for houses because we need to packed and out of our house by April 30 so my mom wants all hands on deck and looking around and getting things packed.

I had mixed feelings when I read his email. First, I thought it was responsible of him to keep me informed of his situation. Second, I considered his request to make up the missed work a step in the right direction. Third, I grimaced at his sentence structure and lack of punctuation or proofreading. As a parent of three (two boys and one girl), I must admit I took issue with the burden placed on him to miss school in order to help the family in an emergency situation. He is a senior. I had been pushing all my students, but especially my seniors to reap the benefits of 12 years of work in the world of academia. I don't believe his mom made the best call. Of course, my position is debatable, but I'm always up for a good debate.

4-18-18

Homelessness? Here?

Received an email inviting teachers to participate in a brainstorming session to discuss addressing the homelessness issue our students are facing. I was surprised that we have this situation. I am aware that it is

116

increasingly prevalent in colleges and universities, but there the homeless crisis is usually the result of parents dropping kids off and encouraging them not to return to their home cities for safety reasons. Here in the public school system, it seems this should be the least of a student's worries. Of course I joined the small team of teachers who were willing to offer up the beginning stages of a solution. What was more heartbreaking is to see that several of my students were on the list of homeless. The next time "he" approaches my desk insisting I share my chips or crackers, I'll know a possible reason for it.

April 18

SHREK

Classroom disruptions are inevitable. They are also annoying, but there are times when we teachers invite them/welcome them, especially today. One of our ESE specialists stopped into my classroom with a student in tow and she inquired about an assignment the student is missing that would boost her F average to a passing grade. I was a tad annoyed by the disruption but accustomed to it from this person, because she cares so much about the students. Reflecting on that encounter reminded me of my first experience with this student. The word I would use to describe her when we first met would be obnoxious (Imagine Shrek in a classroom setting). What I saw standing in the hall today was a nervous student who really, really wants to graduate. Yep, another senior. I'm sharing this with you so that you understand that if a student presents his or her absolute worst side first, that is the only shell they possess. It is the only shell they have because the only thing left to show you is the real them, the vulnerable, the insecure, the real them that can't put their hands on any inkling of esteem. When I'm able to finally see it in my students, the message I'm getting is, I trust you now, Dr. Carter.

April 18
Negative Talk

My students come to me and volunteer academic updates. "I have two D's but I'm doing good in your class." They know that my question is going to be, What are you doing about the D? What is your plan of action to correct it? Even if they complain about the other teacher or they accuse the teacher of pushing their buttons and trying to give them a reason to write a referral (I hear that one a lot), I put it back on them: What is your responsibility? What are you going to do to counter it (the alleged button-pushing)? Have you tried this approach? Have you tried email? Have you spoken to your guidance counselor?

They know I care. They know that care is a no-nonsense-don't-cast-blame brand of ❤.

We are going to take the negative talk, get it out of our system, and, using paper and pen, a talk-through, or a small dry-erase board, we're going to hash out a solution. Drew's situation is above. Anthony's is below.

"I have online math. I'm just not motivated. There really isn't time." All he needed was instruments and he'd have a song. He'd been singing these excuses for so long. "Anthony, you're here with me everyday at lunch. Go now and get it done."

"Okay."

He left and returned half an hour later having spoken to his teacher to plan lunchtime tutoring sessions.

Positive Talk

Marquis approached me after class and enthusiastically commended himself on his reading aloud today. I concurred and he commenced to inform me that he's meeting with his guidance counselor and the fact that he now feels confident that he can get the passing grade this quarter in my class. This is a milestone for Marquis because prior to this, he only engaged in negative self-talk. He was an *occasional* producer and rarely participated.

April 19
Finding Meaning

Domain 1: Planning and Preparation	Domain 2: Classroom Environment
1a - Demonstrating Knowledge of Content and Pedagogy	2a - Creating an Environment of Respect and Rapport
1b - Demonstrating Knowledge of Students	2b - Establishing a Culture for Learning
1c - Setting Instructional Outcomes	2c - Managing Classroom Procedures
1d - Demonstrating Knowledge of Resources	2d - Managing Student Behavior
1e - Designing Coherent Instruction	2e - Organizing Physical Space
1f - Designing Student Assessments	
Domain 3: Instruction	**Domain 4: Professional Responsibilities**
3a - Communicating With Students	4a - Reflecting on Teaching
3b - Using Questioning and Discussion Techniques	4b - Maintaining Accurate Records
3c - Engaging Students in Learning	4c - Communicating with Families
3d - Using Assessment in Instruction	4d - Participating in a Professional Community
3e - Demonstrating Flexibility and Responsiveness	4e - Growing and Developing Professionally
	4f - Showing Professionalism

120

Teachers aspire to receive the level of distinguished during classroom observations. Distinguished means the professional has reached or exceeded demonstrable consistency in each domain (see image, p. 120).

Who gets credit if students pass the re-test? The reading teachers.
The key to distinguished is a website? Perhaps. Teachers feel that they are hard-pressed to create a website; otherwise, they are denied the level of distinguished.

The key to distinguished is a presentation during PLC? Again, according to the teachers, they believe they are denied this acknowledgement because they do not present. Earlier, I mentioned their resentment with having others teach them what they already know when they would rather have fellow teachers present platform discussions.

April 19

Today we used the popcorn style of reading aloud. Students select the next reader and usually ask, "Anybody wanna read next?" Hands always go up or someone will immediately start reading, so no pressure there. Until someone decided to simply call on Steven. He attempted to ignore it. He's already been asked twice to get off his phone, yet continued to watch videos. Somebody called him to read. He had an attitude, looking up and frowning before returning to his video. I called his name; he pretended not to hear me. More positive peer pressure was applied, but he still displayed the nonverbal resistance, and I snapped.

"Look, when you all come in here, whatever you got going on out there [That's exactly how I said it], don't take it out on us. That has nothing to do with us. We have work to do. Your teachers have lives and things going on, but we don't come in here and disrespect you and treat you badly just because of our issues and problems. We have issues and problems, but in here we respect each other and focus on what needs to be done. I pause the reading and discuss passages with you, not for me, but for you, but if you don't want to participate, to have those discussions...(I pause to breathe and in a lower tone, I ask) Who's next?" I was ready to continue reading.

In a whisper, a student near me implores, "Miss I need you to go over what we just read. I don't wanna be lost." "Yeah Miss," chimed in another and then another. Relenting, I began summarizing and all across the room I heard genuine reactions to the smile Gatsby had just given to Carraway.

They understood. Not just the text, but me. The same resister volunteered to read.

Note: I am not suggesting snapping as a technique to alter negative behavior. My version of snapping is more of a lecture that looks and sounds like frustrated care on the brink of tapping out. Students sense the above-and-beyond attachment I have for them and understand what we're doing is important.

April 19

Things No One Told Me

1. There's a sign-in sheet that salaried employees—that is, teachers—have to visit everyday twice a day signing in and signing out. No one told me that that was required. No one told me where it was. I just played follow the leader.

2. There are other pieces of information and data that I can retrieve through a system called iGPS and through Scorecard.

3. Some of our students are homeless.

4. Some of our students are not required to speak/to answer when attendance is called/to participate in class.

5. Some of our students are their own Guardian and contact person in case of emergency

6. What PLC, RIPEs, ... stand for

7. Names of students who receive accommodations

8. Specifics of a student's disability

9. What to expect

10. What is expected (go here to take attendance, the green check above the period means you have accurately taken attendance for that class, attendance is one indicator of many that your record keeping is up to standard; you will be evaluated on your record keeping; recommendations for student placement are voluntary, but they count toward annual evaluations.

11. What to do when there is a drill (fire, tornado, etc.)

12. Lots of makeup tests. Lots.

13. Seventh period assemblies cost 3 dollars, so many students don't attend.

14. If you volunteer to tutor after school you will be asked for proof that you really tutored

students. The request for proof will come after tutoring is complete. "Do you have a sign in sheet?"

15. If there is the need for a grade change, you are expected to write justification for changing a grade from a former teacher's F to a passing grade you did not authorize.

16. If your room is infested with bugs you are to walk to the front desk and write in a notebook for the pest control company. Perhaps this is to limit the amount of spray.

17. Teachers are expected to write self-assessments (these amount to short essays) after unannounced observations.

18. Certain athletes might be called out of class by the coach. I'll have to explain this one.,,

DeMarquis is a football player. I know this because he wrote his process essay on the proper way to execute a drive block. The adults around school all sing his praises: He's a good kid. He's a big ol' sweetheart. He is such a bright kid. D shows a lot of promise, and so on.

One day during third period, he stood up, phone in hand, and asked, "Are we doing anything, Ms?"

"I don't know about you, Mr. Mitchell, but your classmates are working independently on their assignments. And me, I'm just sitting here waiting for something exciting to happen."

"I'm sorry. See (showing me his most recent text message), Coach wants me."

"Hand me your phone." I ask you, what usually occurs when something that is none of the class's business happens at your desk —such as a low-volume conversation with another student? All eyes are trained on the teacher's desk. They watch in disbelief as if their looks are saying, "We dare ya!" I'd much rather they continue working, but that never happens. I began texting the coach: "Hi. This is Dr. Carter. D can leave as soon as he turns in his assignment."
He replied, "Okay, thanks." What in the world? This happened more than once.

My challenge to the Danielson method
1. Brain Drain
2. Odyssey
3. ISS
4. Online courses
5. Remediation requests from guidance counselors by way of students asking if they can turn in the one assignment in Q1 that

can raise a 68 to a C so that a final grade of 27 in Q2 can bring the S1 average to a D- so Rhonda, the absentee Senior, can graduate. Teachers adamantly object to these requests (especially after doing the math) despite admin's vehement insistence that teachers accommodate.

Witch Hunts: We Got Him Fired! (I Want Her Fired)

True stories. Students were continuing a conversation when they walked into my classroom. On more than one occasion, I have observed students making plans to assemble and inform a teacher that he cannot teach and should be fired. "We'll tell him today. He doesn't know what he's doing." Days later, I hear rumors, which are later confirmed, that the teacher in question is gone.

In another situation, I had a student come to me with a complaint. "She thinks she can talk to me any kind of way. I just get right back with her: 'I don't care how many other students like you!' That's what I told her. And I requested a meeting and I'm gonna have her fired. She doesn't need to be here, because she is soooo unprofessional." Another student hears him and interjects:

"She's new. And she's from Philly, so get over it. I like her." He is offended by this comment and retorts, "This is a conversation between me and Dr. Carter. I don't care where she's from. I don't have to tolerate her attitude. And if she says something else to me, I'm coming right back at her." The teacher was fresh out of college, so my advice to him was to allow his mother to do most of the talking in the meeting. I also told him that she, like all of us, needs room to grow.

"If she's fired, how does she learn? How does she get better? How does she look back years from now and say, 'Wow, that was me? I was really green back then. Thanks, you guys, for understanding.'"

He calmed down and said he understood what I was saying. He agreed to let his mom do all the talking.

April 23, 2018

Sammy Forsythe knocked on the door of his teacher's office. Mrs. Shuttlesworth cracked the door just enough to see his face and ask, "How can I help you?"

"I'm here to see Ms. Jones about my grades for last week's assignment that I missed."

"Do you have an appointment?" Mrs. Shuttlesworth asked.

"No, I—"

"Well you need to send an email or call us at her extension and I'll be happy to schedule an appointment for you within the next two weeks."

"But the quarter ends this Friday, and I was trying to get a grade in so that I can pass."

"I'm terribly sorry, but you'll need to schedule an appointment."

Of course, the above anecdote is a product of my imagination. The reality of it all is that teachers are required to hold what are referred to as office hours. These hours are really a part of the lunch break that students are given wherein the teacher implements an open-door classroom policy by either skipping lunch or nibbling on something while trying to have a conversation with students about grades, and missing work, and absences, and behaviors, and parties and any other matters that might come up.

No appointment is necessary, no scheduling is required, no email or telephone call prior to arrival. There is no way to call in the first place.

April 25, 2018

Danielson is treated as the district's end-all-be-all of best practices in teaching and learning, and with good reason. But such an approach functions best in an environment where teachers and students are on one accord and external factors are at a minimum. That is not the case in many of our public schools today.

The problem as I see it: Treating learning as an after thought. Attendance is not monitored or addressed. Referrals are treated like a classroom hiatus. Remediation is a catch phrase holding absolutely no value and lacking justification. Weekly, teachers are telling students they must sign and abide by a contract. Some students are sent to ask for remediation for which they do not qualify. Qualify: 49% or higher in a quarter. Students come in with zero percent and perfect attendance. So let's paint the picture: Jay is present Monday through Friday. Each day, students are assigned a laptop from the mobile computer cart. Jay gets a computer, logs in, and pulls up the assigned site. He works on the assignment each day. On Friday the teacher tells the class its time to print. Jay doesn't go to the library to print. He says he doesn't have the ten cents per page. He reluctantly shares this information after the teacher expresses repeated urgency. The teacher seeks assistance from the ESE support person. He works with Jay, but Jay shrugs his shoulders when asked where the file is. The following week, teachers are emailed instructions to pick up envelopes filled with midterm progress reports for distribution during 4th period. Some of these reports are attached to a letter for parents. The letters further illuminate areas needing improvement (F in Geo, F in US His, etc.) " Jay needs to do xyz. He is not on track to graduate. Most parents respond to teacher emails and phone calls but never have I seen one alarmed-or-concerned- parent request for a conference as a result of the progress report.

Achievement should be viewed from a point of excellence. Dress code is mentioned in the morning announcements. Being on time is mentioned in emails and announcements. The overlooked correlation is the allowance to walk the halls on their phones. The allowance to sag the uniformed pants, boys, and (yes) some girls. Students sit and watch the clock or make advance requests to "go to the bathroom 10 minutes after the tardy bell." They know the "no sag" rule just as well. They know the "no cell phone" rule just as well. The referral is garbage. It means nothing to a student who needs a nap. Nothing to a student who, upon return from a day off after a referral, has 10 more school days to sleep or watch a movie on his phone before mom can make her way to the teacher-requested conference.

So, so, so many online platforms for teaching, and planning and resource consumption. Colleges have 1. Student evaluation of instruction and 2. Peer Classroom observations. Public schools have Self Assessments, Announced classroom observation, Unannounced classroom observations, requirements to submit evidence to justify scoring yourself Distinguished, and rumors among faculty that limits are set cn the # of Distinguished and Proficient a YPET administrator can assign to any one instructor.

College professors go through a similar rigor during what is called Tenure and Promotion. Public school teachers in some districts no longer benefit from the security of tenure. So tell me again, why is Danielson the last word in teaching and learning?

This, among other things, sets professors apart from public school teachers. This is also why my re-entry into the system to remedy a shortage crisis should have been approached with my experience and credentials in mind.

The state requires that we teach certain novels over the course of a school year. If a teacher deviates from the assigned text, s/he must indicate a match that satisfies the same requirements as the original. Another limitation. Sure, we want to make sure teachers aren't assigning *Mad Magazine, Archie* or *Junie B Jones* for high school juniors, but sometimes students need variety, especially if their reading is grades below level. I taught at a high school where my senior athletes admitted they had never finished a novel they started. To match interest level, reading level, and my novel completion goals for each student, I assigned a total of four different titles to one class. J.D. Salinger, William Golding, George Orwell and Ray Bradbury had my students thinking, reacting, journaling, and questioning the worlds and characters they created. One book wasn't enough.

April 23, 2018

Students in Brain Drain are given a set number of weeks to complete an assignment. Some of us draft contracts when we go back and review the information from the quarter in question, look at their grades, look at which assignments are summatives, review that with the student, get signatures from the student and parent, and then provide them with the school designated deadlines to complete those assignments. All of that, and some students still don't submit any work, but they're graduating seniors.

April 23

K. M. Watched as we scampered trying to rid ourselves of very large roaches in the room. He saw that I was a bit distraught at the location of the roaches, which disrupted a lot of what I was doing in my work area, so he walked over to me and began to sympathize. He commented on how disappointing it is that students were eating in the classroom. You see, he had drawn a cause-and-effect analysis and knew also that the solution would be to stop eating in the classroom. K.M. had gone from what I observed at our initial encounter to a student who could leave his area, walk over to me, be considerate of my concerns, express his disappointment with student behavior, assess the situation and conclude the cause, and then and comment on what he knew the solution was. I was thoroughly impressed.

4-25-18

A Safe Place to "be"

'A' came to 4th period wearing dangling hands from his ear lobes. "A, I'm afraid your new look is something I'm going to have to get used to. A is an unassuming, constantly smiling young man who went from struggling academically and saying little, to daily volunteering to read, asking many probing questions (to the extent his mind will allow such probing) and wearing earrings, a choker and just a hint of lip gloss. Deep-voiced, smiling A.

He has not, like M sat down with me at lunch and shared. M had a huge fight with his mom because he told her he is gay. I could tell it was a statement made for the first time by the sheer repetition. M is also a self-professed clairvoyant. I warned him to guard his spirit, for there is an apparent (at least apparent to me) sensitivity to it.

Then there are Brooke and Justyne. Brooke shared her preference during BHM when students were permitted to choose topics. Ru Paul was in high demand 3rd period. Justyne asked to dress like a man for her novel-character assignment.
Not one of these kids asked my opinion. No one was curious about how I might feel about their preferences. Whether I agreed or accepted them. They passed the threshold of assuming and entered directly into the realm of knowing. They somehow knew that whatever my personal opinions or even my strong beliefs might be, I cared for and respected them as human beings, as individuals, and I had made it each person's obligation to show the same respect toward their peers.

One of the many impromptu speeches that I make is below: Class, I need us to keep something in mind. Sometimes, you speak in low tones so that I can't hear what you're saying. But when you talk to the two or three people in your immediate vicinity, remember that other people can hear you as well. Whatever you're saying might be funny to your friends, but it might make someone else who hears it uncomfortable. Don't let your friends' laughter cause any confusion. Funny doesn't necessarily mean appropriate or acceptable. There is a time and a place for everything. This classroom may not be the place. And on rare occasions, the time for certain conversations is never.

Teachers have to have eyes in the backs of their heads and elephant ears in order to maintain order (and some semblance of peace and quiet) and safety in the classroom.
A safe place to become.

April 25

I wasn't going to share this, but what the heck. It is important that you know how quickly a student can go from hot to cold, from docile to defiant in a matter of minutes. Diego was a talkative student among other talkative students. He once explained that this was due to his culture. Okay. On most days, Diego has needed constant redirection, even to get him to take his seat. He expresses himself better standing. Diego, have a seat. Diego, lower your voice. Diego, get to work; you only have ___ minutes to finish this. Diego, Diego, Diego. On two occasions, Diego visited me during lunch to discuss his grades. The first such encounter was unpleasant, but served as a harbinger

137

for the second, and again for the final in-class fracas. "Hi, Ms. I mean Dr. Carter. I need to talk to you about my grade. I need you to explain to me why I have a D. I should have a B in this class, man." Now, based on the words, "I need you to explain" I am already not a fan of this particular encounter.

"Well, let's take a look at Scorecard. You're missing the self-reflection essay, the Scavenger Hunt and –

"No, I did that. I completed that and turned it in."

"Okay, well since you interrupted me, I'm not sure which assignment you're referring to."

"I'm re-fer-ring [that's how he said it; he stressed the word as if to make his point perfectly clear] to the self-reflection essay. I turned that in." He is now standing. This encounter would take too long to relive in text, so I'll just wrap it up by saying I had to put my foot down: "You are the same student who came to me last quarter accusing me of losing your work, raising your voice and expressing such great concern for your grade. I have urged you before to always check Scorecard for your grades. You continue to wait until the last minute to show concern. Since you found the missing work in your backpack the last time, I suggest you check there again this time."

You must understand how important it is for a teacher of my stature (average height and weighing in at a buck 30) to alter the course when headed down the wrong track with an irate student. I never lose sight of the fact that I make the final decision. I decide when the volume should be lowered; I decide when the conversation should be postponed for a better time; I decide how to resolve an issue. It is a positive form of control that keeps everyone on the right track.

May 1

Bellringer
Lots of talkative students on one side of the classroom. Surely they have the bellringer completed. It is the first time I choose not to time them (5 minutes).
...T if you are not on task tomorrow, I'm going to trade shoes with you and let you try walking from desk to desk in a lady's size 8 heel.

"That's crazy though, 'cause I do wear a size 8," said a lone male student seated near the taller size 11-wearing athletes.

May 2

"Good morning Dante. Come with me."
Once inside the classroom, he asked, "Do you have a paper towel?" "Yes, right over there."
Pointing toward the door, he had just killed a roach.
"Thank you, ewe, etc." Once he was settled and finished with the hand sanitizer, I asked, "Do you write or type faster?" He still didn't know why I had invited him into the classroom before the first period bell.
"Type."
"Ok, grab a computer. You're going to type the summaries once I load the information on the screen for you."
Without hesitation or resistance, he grabbed a laptop and waited for the words to appear on the screen. Dante volunteers nothing in the way of academia, so when he was ready for me to advance the screen, he simply sat quietly and glanced only halfway behind him in my direction. Once I saw the signals, I advanced and he commenced working again. Seventeen minutes after the bell rang. I was afraid he would stop working in front of

the others so I distracted each arrival with small talk and eventually offered some computers for a variety of important reasons. Dante looked around. Seeing four unevenly distributed computers seemed to allow him to commence working. Sigh

May 2

Older student-males need teacher-females to allow them to exhibit their masculinity, express themselves and make mistakes.
I told the same student from yesterday that I brought a pair of size eights. He responded with boisterous enthusiasm in defense of his chatter. "I'm thirsty miss. I have to finish my water. I'm not talking." He finally got to work.

May 3

Becka walked in late and smiling, as if she had just done me a favor by arriving. I broke the silence in my classroom with: "You want them to separate us." In a voice of desperation, I repeated, "They are going to separate us!"
"Who, Ms!?"
"The Discipline office. When I write the referral for your excessive tardies, we will be apart." She relaxed, smiled and understood.

The next day, she arrived early and walked over to me.

We exchanged a loud high-five!
May 4

Perception

The committee to address student homelessness in the school convened and the following comment was made by a member. "Teachers have lost touch and don't realize what these students are going through. They need to be more sensitive to these students and be more caring."

Hmm. Are you cringing?

May 4

Emails to Motivate

Please know your YPET evaluators will be copied on all emails regarding inaccurate attendance and this process falls under 4b (Maintaining Accurate Records) and can be reflected on your YPET evaluation as documentation. [I'd much rather be told why attendance is so critical. This sounds like I'm being grounded for coming in after curfew.]

May 8

Breakthroughs

Dante has been coming in to sit with me just a few minutes before class. No particular reason. Today, he caught me off guard and began a long descriptive discussion of the game he spends (too much) time playing on his phone.

He stopped sleeping in class and being on his phone during instruction a long time ago. So today was special in that, it was his first time initiating a conversation with me. The first time he ever shared something that he enjoys unrelated to course work.

He still owes himself a process essay (his recipe for Russian waffles). He wrote and even showed me the outline and rough draft but never turned anything in (insert frowny face here).

As he explained the game to me this morning, all I could think about was audio recording him. Students like Dante can use voice-to-text to write their essays. Sigh...

5-8-2018

<u>PLC</u>

In our meeting, teachers again lamented the advent of Brain Drain. One teacher even commented on how she deals with students who need to make up work because they can't be trusted. They cheat. They get the information from other students. So if it's a multi-page test, she has them come up and take one page at a time and complete it. It's a shame it's come to that.

One teacher shared how she feels it is unfair that a white student who needs <u>additional</u> accommodations does not qualify because she's not black. I doubt there was a document with the requirement "must be black" but she somehow concluded that the only race qualifying for this particular accommodation is Black.

I think it was an appeal to me because of my race and perhaps to a lesser degree, the PhD that I hold.

When I was asked if I had any information I'd like to share in our report to the principal, I told them that the problems I heard expressed in this meeting take me back to my original position regarding the curriculum framework and how so much of what teachers are teaching is formulaic. We've forgotten that writing is a process. They agreed and added that teaching argumentative writing at the early part of the year is a mandated mistake.

They also expressed their disappointment and lack of faith in intensive reading for juniors and seniors. I then shared my surprise to even find that such a thing exists and that it is needed a full year for students who are in regular classes. One teacher shared that her students who are in Advanced Placement and Honors cannot pass the SSA, which is a state-mandated assessment. Even as I write this I gasp, shake my head and wonder about the fate, or by some miracle destiny, of our students and the education system.

I want to pause briefly from journaling and offer some insights into why first-year teachers, novices and sometimes even the seasoned educators stick so religiously to the curriculum guide. I want to share it because one of the Professionals in the room suggested that they don't do enough outside of the map to wholly educate and fully prepare our students. Allow me to examine this based on my consultative experiences in other teachers' classrooms.

The Curriculum Map is the Dry Bones of Instruction

When a teacher is given a schedule, it includes what time to arrive at school, what time the first bell rings, when planning is scheduled and how much time is allotted for lunch. Teachers must accomplish predetermined tasks within a certain time frame. The same applies to instruction. The Curriculum Guide or Map includes standards, learning targets for students to reach, proposed timelines for units of instruction, and even specific pages in the textbook they must cover. This, coupled with the actual lesson plan, is often referred to as Scope and Sequence. If a teacher wishes to study a particular novel, s/he must get permission to do so and make sure the novel in question satisfies the guidelines set forth in the Curriculum Guide. The adopted textbook even includes guidance along the margins telling teachers what to say and when to say it.

For a new or limited-experienced teacher, the goal is to do things right. To be asked back next year. Over time, a teacher who has adhered so strictly to the map has made it a habit. It has become the way to prepare lessons where there is no room or time for supplementation. And as I learned in a conversation with another principal the other day, each school leader applies a different weight to the burden of following the Map or Guide and assessing based on standards. Teachers want to do it right. They want to be asked back.

I look at the Curriculum Map as a skeleton, not a fully fleshed body. It merely delineates for me what the state and district has determined will be the measure of achievement for students at various levels. During my planning, I take the items that are required and place them in one category. I take the optional items and select which will align well with my way of teaching, the various learning styles I anticipate, and their current levels. As a first-year teacher, I began curating items I could make a permanent member of my arsenal (the marrow). Now, I have a laundry list of projects, activities, games, tests, quizzes, outings, and community advocates I can pull from to enhance the learning experience for my students (the flesh and pulse). My bar is always set higher than the state's. I am in the trenches. I know what they need and I know what they can handle.

For teachers who struggle with classroom management, none of the aforementioned will facilitate learning. If discipline, distractions, and disrespect are the top three topics every day, there will never be time or space for differentiated instruction. Teachers need room to grow, to be creative. They need academic freedom with the Map as their, well, compass, but, if the Map is introduced as a mandated tool from which teachers cannot deviate, far too many teachers will inadvertently conform to a one-size-fits-all approach. When that happens, we spend tax-payer dollars trying to solve problems money created.

As I said at the beginning of this book, teachers are the first line; they are in the trenches.

5/9/18

Remember the bright young lady who had to retake the exam due to unacceptable commentary? You remember. Rutabaga. Chefs refer to her as a rather strong turnip. She graded papers for me today. Her coming around was gradual and in true stewed rutabaga fashion. She started by joining fellow classmates on my side of the room and talking to them. She possesses excellent social skills, able to strike up a conversation with anyone about anything, from the silly to the serious (is water wet? If I eat myself will I get fat?) She transitioned from that to sitting closer and closer to my desk but only until the tardy bell rang. Suddenly she went from shaking her head, No and smiling in reply to my requests for work, to proving my earlier verbal prediction that she was an A student, still with the same defiance in her smile. How did she get around to grading papers?

1. By offering me a green pen to replace my pencil. I ignored the request since I had a green pen of my own stashed in the desk drawer.

2. By pointing out an error in Item 16 on the Answer Key

3. By walking away and returning with her green pen.

She earned an A on the test, by the way.

May 16

Hello Poochie,

Making the move from traditional teacher development to a competency-based approach using micro-credentials is not a simple leap of faith — rather it's a process of changing the status quo. It's a shift from hours to outcomes — from simply showing up to learning by doing.

At the School District of South Milwaukee, their director of instruction, Dr. Ann Newman, calls it a journey down the pathway to success. Below you can learn more about their journey and how they aligned the right incentives to make it a success.

Best,
Sanford Kenyon
CEO, BloomBoard

When I read the preceding email, I was offended. I know, I should have treated it like all the other emails a teacher receives in the course of a day, but certain words leapt out of the page and slapped me in the face. Was Sanford saying teachers simply show up in order to get the in-service hours? That the only way to eliminate this status-quo sort of thinking is through micro-credentials? Moving on.

May 21

From: Andrea Seggano Serarra
<andreaserarra0218@gmail.com>
Sent: Friday, May 18, 2018 9:17 PM
To: Carter, Poochie
Subject: Thank-you letter

Dear Dr. Carter

I wanted to thank you for being one of the best teachers I've ever had throughout my high school years. When I first came into your class I was so scared because I thought it was going to be very hard for me, since my first language is not English, and also that it was going to be hard for me to get along with your class. I thought I was going to struggle but you were always there to help me with anything and that's why I am grateful with you. For me to come in the middle of the year with a not perfect writing, reading and, speaking of English was a huge challenge but with your help I managed to beat the challenge. I was always asking questions because I wanted everything to be correct and sometimes I thought it was annoying for me to be asking so much but you never gave me a "you're being annoying" attitude. Dr. Carter you're great and passionate on what you do. You're also a wonderful person and a huge motivation, I always saw you as a wise woman. I wanted to thank you for making me feel welcome and for teaching me so much. I will miss you a lot and I will always remember you, you have a place in my heart.

Thank you for everything
With gratitude
Andrea Seggano Serarra

There's so much I need to share that has transpired in the past couple of weeks. I'll try to get back to it, particularly the contributions made by the students when we covered our summative activity for *The Great Gatsby* party. But today I want to talk about Devin, who asked me why we have to read and why we have to read novels. Although I gave him a shortened answer to the question, I want to expound on it a little more here. If a 7th grader were to ask you, Devin, why you have to finish a novel you should be able to support the importance of reading a novel from start to finish and not finding yourself lost or confused in the process even if the author is telling a story or several stories within a story. If you're not lost, if you're not confused, if you can identify that strategy, if you recognize allegory, cause and effect, simile, metaphor, personification, any relationship to the real world—especially if it's fiction—then you understand why novels are so important. What message did you get from it? What things did you pull from it that the author did not intend, and what things did you miss that the author had hoped you would find? Critical thinking comes into play. When you had a question the author did not answer for you, what did you do to get the answers you sought? Short stories like Saki's "The Open Window" or Jamaica Kincaid's "Girl" provide for deep thinking and expanded thought, a bit of entertainment and a lesson or two. Nevertheless, the novel calls on the mind to assemble characters, places and events—sometimes in order of occurrence, sometimes, because of flashback, out of order as in E.B. White's "Once More to the Lake" (a short story, by the way)—and, completing the reading, leave that story (or those stories) with a lesson, a message, a greater understanding of the world we live in, or at least a sense of excitement about the author-created world you discovered.

5 22 2018
No Excuses

It is apparent to me that my students who are rising seniors are accustomed to having teachers come up with alternative assignments when they don't come prepared. I'm not that teacher. Today they were asked to come to school without their backpacks—in keeping with a commonly-held practice—because we're nearing the end of the school year. They made little fusses the day before and I told them they do this every year; this is nothing new. You have arms and you have elbows, so you can carry anything that you need in your hands without the use of your backpack. Still, many of them came to school today without even paper or pen or pencil. We had an essay assignment today after watching a 5-minute video titled, Is College Worth It? with Tucker Carlson. My students looked around and saw that they were in the majority when it came to who did not have paper or pencil.

At one point I think I was heard clear across the hallway as I stood, held up my book bag and stacks of papers and said, "This is what I have to do at the end of the year. This is what I take home at the end of the year. This is what I bring back with me everyday. So your coming in here and telling me you don't have paper and a writing utensil because you weren't allowed to bring your *backpack* is ridiculous and pathetic! You have 30 seconds before I hit play on this video and you need to be prepared to take notes!" Suddenly, the students became extremely resourceful, each with a piece of paper on his or her desk and ready to take the necessary notes in order to write an effective opinion paper.

If we hold students accountable without excuse, they will deliver. They were proud of the papers that they wrote.

We discussed the importance of using effective hooks/starters to introduce the topic. I warned them that as big boys and girls we do not use starters or hooks that repeat the title as our introduction. Is College Worth It is not an appropriate hook, because it is the topic of conversation. So it pushed them to remember what they learned and to demonstrate that knowledge. Here's an example: "Have you ever heard the saying, boys go to Jupiter and get more stupider. Girls go to college and get more knowledge? Not anymore. College has become the new grown-ups kindergarten with students spending more time eating, shopping and partying, while only 2.6 hours are spent studying..." or this one "Imagine you pay hundreds of thousands of dollars to go to college. It's been two years since you started your academic journey. Your grades are looking good; you even have a high GPA of 3.8. Then you realize you haven't learned anything. All that money spent and your knowledge didn't even expand. Ask yourself, is college worth it?"

The former writer started with a question. The latter began with an anecdote and drew the reader in even further with a question that mirrors the topic. They are learning to take control of their writing and to not worry so much about whether it will be good enough.

5-22-18

A number of things always stand out when we have our 4-person PLC (professional learning communities) meetings. We discuss the same issues with standardized testing, the same issues with Brain Drain, the same issues with the Danielson method.

The district calculates values for assignments. The teacher must keep that in mind when planning. I found this out in May. When is the school year over? May.

In the May 22 meeting, Ms. Dee was extremely passionate about credit. She insisted that no one teacher should ever take the credit for any strides a student makes. "I would never dare say that I alone was responsible for the success of any student! It

is a collaborative effort. The scores they get on an assessment can be attributed to more than one person." I wasn't sure where this was coming from, as it seemed to fall on her from somewhere above. I couldn't trace it back to any previous statement any one of us had made. I have heard that reading teachers, not English teachers, are credited for the success of students on Language Arts assessments.
I'm sharing it here to offer you my point of view.

Her name was Mrs. Eubanks. She was my 9th grade teacher. She was solely responsible for many things in my 12-year-old life. She impressed me, even then, with her ability to pace instruction based on her ready assessment of her entire class's need to have her re-teach a thing or to move us onward and upward. I still remember many things she taught us and carried those lessons with me onto my college campus of choice. There were other teachers who shared responsibility for my smooth transition into college life and post secondary rigor, but those folks entered the stage in 10th, then 11th, then 12th grade. Mrs. Eubanks was solely responsible for the student I was proud to be as a high school freshman. I credit her and her alone.

5-22-18

Voice-to-text

Some ESE students feel extremely burdened when given writing assignments. The key is to maximize a strategy I shared with Alexander Vella. He had good ideas for his essay assignment but struggled with putting pen to paper. He is not the only one who has this issue.

I asked him if he had a phone. He and I stepped into the hall with our cellular devices and I walked him through accessing his email.

He followed the steps I took on my phone, inputting my name in the Recipient box and then clicked on the microphone icon. I spoke into mine as he spoke into his. What you see below is what he has so far. I explained to him that this is the equivalent of writing an essay.
He could only do it if I stood next to him or gave him privacy out in the hall, not in front of classmates (smile).

From: Alexander Vella
<alexuozh@yahoo.com>
Sent: Tuesday, May 22, 2018 10:19 AM
To: Carter, Poochie
Subject: Is college worth it

Why would we go to college if they are lower standards. The prices are colleges are rising while education is falling. cord to Carson "2.6 hours spent studying they spend more time drinking shopping and party

Al spent considerable time trying to make edits as he dictated. When I saw this, I told him that what I do is repeat the words I intended and make changes later, as it saves time and allows the train of thought to continue down the track.

5-23-18

There was a time many years ago when I would insist that my students speak when spoken to even if being passed in the hallway or greeted in a cafeteria. In the time that I've spent at this school, I've come to realize these students have so many different kinds of issues and so many different kinds of struggles that they don't know how to muster a hello, so I reached the point where I would just speak to them knowing they would not return the salutation. Gradually, I saw a change in about 90% of those who initially would not speak, would not even make eye contact now making eye contact, now approaching my desk, now speaking in return. We are working with a different population these days. We must be sensitive to who they are and why they are the way they are. They are in a cocoon of sorts, and prying them out of it would do to them what it would to a caterpillar.

5-23-18

Zach

He spoke today.
Entering the classroom. I stood greeting my students and the one I worried about, the one I would see walking alone during lunch, but never eating, the one who seemed to have not one friend, walked up to the door.
"Hi Zach."
"Hi."
He participated in an online spelling game on Monday. He did not raise his hand. He just looked at me.
"You wanna try this one, Zach?"
He nodded.
"Okay, go. Shhh." I quieted the others.
He, of course, spelled the word correctly.
But today he greeted me. He made eye contact and greeted me.

In class, he came empty-handed like
most. "Josh, I have your essay. Did you
complete the graphic organizer?"
"No, ma'am."
"Okay, it's a separate grade."
"Oh. Is it alright if I complete it now?"
"Sure."
"Zach, (holding up his essay), I have your
essay. Did you complete the graphic
organizer?"
He shook his head.
"It's a separate grade. Can I get you to
complete it now?"
Nodding, he stood to approach my desk.
"Can I borrow a pencil?"
I gladly obliged.
Some of my entries are difficult to type
through tears. Tears of joy and tears of
uncertainty.
I am filled with joy when I see such
breakthroughs.
I am, however uncertain about my place
here next year. I came here with a plan.
Teach, prepare students for state and district
assessments, and less than a year later, go
back to consulting full time.
But as my daughter warned, something
happened.
I became attached. Not even in the sense
that I had in the past. This attachment is new
to me. I find myself attached to the degree of

success these kids will realize now that
we've made some strides, gotten so far.
Together.

> "Dr. Carter, you're the only one who
> cares."
> "Dr. Carter, can you request
> students? I want you to request
> me."
> "You comin' back next year, Ms?"
> "That's my plan." (I didn't want to tell
> them No.)
> "Well I wanna take your
> class."

The seniors are all done.
Some barely made it. They were diagnosed
with an acute case of Senioritis.
Others were just feeling burnout. One such
student sent me an email:
Another gave me a card: "Thank you for
preparing me for college."
I don't want the rising seniors to lose what
they have found. Some have found their
voices. Others their confidence. Still others
have found a love of learning.
Should I be concerned about what will
become of them if I don't return?

5-24-18

What do you do when you have options?
One minute I'm dead set on returning here;
the next I'm ready to walk away fed up with
procedure, because I look so far into the
future of these kids and it frustrates me to
see how they are exempt from
consequences or allowed to take a small
situation to its extreme. So today I go from
100 to 10, from Tommy to Kriss, who walks
in during lunch and shows me the cake he
baked in culinary. As he walks away, he
says, "I just came by to say hi." He
happened to be in the same classroom with
Tommy and watched that whole
unnecessary drama unfold. I went from
being done and ready to make other
arrangements for next year away from this
high school to wondering, "Why did he come
in here and change my mind?" Does that
make me fickle? Definitely fed up.

5-24-18

Different. In an Undervalued Sort of Way

This is where I think the teaching profession
differs from others. Teachers encounter and
engage with over 100 personalities per day
and must, not should, must give 100% of

themselves because, like doctors, we have lives in our hands. Like lawyers, we hold futures in our hands, and like firefighters, we have to be mindful of our and their surroundings and potential hazards that may not be apparent at first glance. Like police officers, we must be skilled at and ready to de-escalate a situation for the safety of all present.

While doing all these things, we still must keep teaching and learning at the center of it all, not just for a few but for every student, engaging them the entire period or block each and every day. And even though counseling is discouraged and parenting is reserved for their first teacher, some students don't care about those boundaries; therefore, the teacher can easily become counselor, therapist, mediator, advisor, mom or Auntie, dad or uncle. Students make those decisions and with careful approach, the shrewd teacher can/does wear the hat the student places on his head without overstepping boundaries of professionalism, ethics or unfettered influence. The fluctuation between leaving and staying is not isolated to me. If she were of retirement age, this could have been Patty Lace's last year.

Is there an ideal way to remove a disruptive kid from the classroom? Not a disruptive kid who responds to redirection; the kid who refuses to respond to redirection, the kid who had a schedule change because he's been accused of threatening to "f*ck up" another teacher. Is there an ideal way to remove that child? The expectation is that the teacher pause instruction, write a referral, send the student with referral in hand trusting that that student will make his or her way to the discipline office, and then continue with instruction. I have yet to meet a teacher who finds this process to be ideal, or appropriate, or reasonable, or logical, or sensible. Ideally, the student should be sent out with just a simple teeny tiny piece of colorful paper that is designed to be a pre-referral to get them out of the room. The referral should subsequently follow, reaching the discipline office no later than the end of the occurrence period. It should not be an interruption. What happens at this school is, well, I'll give you today's example. Student demanded, with profanity, that I give him something to write with as if it is my job. The F bomb is not welcome here. I walked across the hall and requested the aid of a male teacher who escorted the student half way to the discipline office. Within minutes, someone to whom I have never been

introduced walked in, stopped at the entrance and waited for eye contact. I was reading the exam instructions and passage to the class. Her walkie-talkie went off. She thought nothing of it. I was now half way through prepping my students for the final. She took a few more steps in. I continued reading. A few more steps. I turned the page. "Do you have the referral?"
Huh? These kids can't afford the slightest cognitive interruption during a literary moment. But alas, I have been interrupted. "I'm writing it once they start their finals."
By the way, during lunch, I saw that same student who actually called to me to let me know that he got a pen that he needed from his second period teacher before his second period exam and sarcastically stated, Now that wasn't so hard was it?"
P. S. Another entry needs to address the buzzers in our classrooms. The buzzers that do not work. In case of emergency.

May 25, 2018

Abuse (not *of*, *by* the student)

In the world of welfare or subsidies or state assistance or aid, those receiving it fall into two categories: they either really need the help and follow procedures and steps to the letter, or they've learned how to manipulate and abuse the system. In the world of higher education, financial aid serves the purpose of providing the opportunity for a student who could not otherwise pay for courses toward a certificate or degree. To be able to do so, these people fall into two categories: those who follow the steps and utilize those funds appropriately-- and even sometimes returning any refunds, any surplus amounts, or they learn the system and milk it (pass or fail), and abuse it by going shopping with any surplus, or pay rent, or travel or party.

In the public school system, at least here where I am, students aren't familiar with certain terms. They are, however, very familiar with DIA, SAT, extended time, Brain Drain and their favorite, remediation. They don't know about learning targets; they couldn't tell you where one is located on the board or on the wall or in the ceiling or on the floor for that matter. That aspect of the educational process is unimportant and insignificant. The weakest word for them is referral; the second weakest word is ISS, which stands for in-school suspension. The repeat offenders are not concerned with any consequences. It is merely time off, a mini vacay. If you walk past the room where all ISS students are corralled, you will find them sitting in chairs, not desks, holding cell phones, not books, biding their time learning nothing, just like it was in the classroom right before they misbehaved. Are they monitored, you ask? Well, of course. The person monitoring them sits at a desk and does only God knows what.

The immediate reaction from some will be, well what do you expect him to do? Babysit? Teach all subjects represented at one time? I can only answer that question based on my own experience. When I was responsible for this position at a different school we didn't have a cell phone issue, but I certainly would have restricted any cell phone use and I would've given them all the same assignment, an essay. They would've been required to write whatever teacher's name they were going to be missing. I would've given them a life-lesson type of essay assignment or an SAS game: what have you learned in school this week? or what has been your most significant learning experience and in what class? Be specific. Provide dates. Something! Use your phone to define the following 20 words—something!

May 29

We just returned from Memorial Day weekend. We are reaching the close of the day. The last day of school is tomorrow. Tomorrow. Students have completed six out of seven scheduled exams. The last one is tomorrow morning at 7:29 a.m. So, why is it I'm getting this email?

Tayji, Munroe Y.S.

Today, 1:10 PM
Hey Dr. Carter,

Is there anything Sebastia can to do to improve her grade for quarter 4?

Thank you,

My response:

Hello.

Not at this point. She and I have gone back and forth about assignments when she chose to be on her phone. Mrs. Taylor has pulled her aside several times and I even involved her dad at one point. Even after warning her that there would be no making up work she simply chose not to do, she would continue to make poor choices.

By the way, she and I just spoke about this 10 minutes ago. If not people, she needs to at least learn to respect time.

Moments later, Sebastia walked into my classroom without a pass to inform me that she had a message from Mrs. Raynier, who wanted to know if there was anything Sebastia could do to raise her grade. "Really? I just got an email from your guidance counselor asking if there was anything you could do raise your grade this quarter."

"Oh no, I didn't know that."
"Yeah. I told her about the warnings I gave you. Do you remember? I told you that when the day came and you asked me if you could now do work that you simply chose not to do in here, when you finally decided at the last minute that you feel like completing the work, I wouldn't take the time to go over anything with you. I wouldn't take the time to add grading your work to my existing stack of exams. I told her we had involved your mom, Mrs. Taylor and even taken your cell phone, so the lesson should have been learned the last two times I gave you a

chance. Once I warned you about how this day would look, you should have chosen a better option. I am a woman of my word" A student walked up as I was finishing my statement.

"Hello, how are ya? What can I do for you?"

Sebastia walked away and began a pleasant conversation on her way out, as if nothing had happened between us. There's always summer school, Odyssey, Brain Drain, something hiding under the guise of remediation.

Why am I so hard on remediation? Some students truly need remediation and if they can prove mastery, why not give them the chance? Here's why:

Dustin arrives to class during lunch for remediation. During the entire 45 minutes, he sits blankly and completes maybe one sentence or one math problem. Right before the bell rings, he asks, "Can I finish this at home?" or "Can I finish this tomorrow?" or "Can I finish this in Ms. Hazard's class?" Translation: Can I take this with me so my friend can do the work for me? I don't know what the hell I'm doing; I just need a grade.

In Sebastia's case, she has figured out the math. If there are a total of 15 assignments in the span of a quarter and she's missing 7 of them, why complete them if in Remediation, she can complete 1 of the assignments—a summative—raise the failing grade to a D and continue to ignore the other 6 assignments.

I explained to another student today that this is not a buffet. You see, he wanted to pick and choose which classes he would attend and which teachers he would avoid. The same applies to students who are only interested in completing what they have been told are Summatives, avoiding the measly formatives altogether. "So, Ji, you want chocolate covered marshmallows and frozen custard, but you're not interested in the corn and pasta?

May 29

Teachers say the darndest things.

1. Kids, if you don't want administrators on you about being out of class, just keep moving. Don't stop and talk. Keep walking around. That's all it takes at SeaWalk High School.

2. We're babysitting. These last few days, we aren't' doing anything but babysitting these kids.

May 31, 2018

I just went back and read the Jan 8 entry and was blown away. I had forgotten these were the same kids! What a change, what a difference a few months make. Yesterday, we said goodbye and I cried privately as I watched them make their way to school buses and cars, some walking home. I prayed a prayer for them and thanked God for the opportunity to meet these kids. One by one. I have never felt such a longing to pick up where we left off. I never felt that my work was not done. This feels incomplete. What if I'm not here when they come back? What if they walk in and don't see me? I comfort myself by saying, "They will find someone who fits the bill. It'll be okay." Then I remember Wendy's words, "They were lucky you agreed to come here. They couldn't get anybody to take this job!"

I'm sitting at my desk at home thinking about my conversation with my 4th period and I hear Steve's voice. "Do you lose sleep like that, Ms?"

"I lost sleep like that this morning. I was up at 4 angry that I could not go back to sleep, thinking of ways to reach some of you, to help some of you, to teach you things that interest you and still cover what is required that you say doesn't interest you." It has been months since I've lost sleep. Months since I've laid awake wondering what or how or if. I still had a few I needed more time with, but I had reached them.

Where do I go from here?
I want to return and continue working with the students. They worked very hard for me and for themselves. They are ready to continue the work. I feel torn between the tough hurdles teachers must surmount in order to gain eligibility and to remain credentialed. It is the same for the seasoned, experienced teacher-trainer as it is for the young college graduate with only an internship under his belt. I am considering the time it will take to complete the many requirements to return vs. the option to take on an administrative position outside the district wherein I might have a greater impact by training other teachers to develop skills and incorporate my methods and strategies on a grand scale. Do I return so that we save a few or leave so that we save many? I know the few and have developed intimate

relationships with many of them (even a few I don't teach) and even the scantily spoken words with the quiet ones whom I respect deeply. We need more teachers like Wendy and Tobias and James and Judy. Our teachers need the freedom to teach, really teach. There is a way to strike a balance between checks and balances and ample training and effective, distinguished teaching. We are sacrificing one for the other.

One of my junior consultants submitted, on my behalf, the following content in a 2-minute video for a TED Talk opportunity.

5,4,3,2,1,...Lift Off!

The New York Post published an article on May 26, 2018 titled, "Deadbeat Son is a Sign of America's Failure to Raise Boys." *A judge in New York ruled that a 30-year-old man must move out of his childhood home on June 1 after his parents served him with several notices asking him to go.*

Background: Mark and Christina Rotondi decided to remove their son from the family phone plan. We can surmise he had been on the plan for at least 13 years. He was also provided money to move out and start a new life, but he spent that money on other things.

The article references *Failure to Launch,* a 2006 romantic comedy. I hadn't seen that movie, but I had seen *Step Brothers*, a 2008 comedy depicting the wayward, sluggish lives of two adult males who were also still living at home. Pew Research conducted a poll that revealed men ages 18 to 36 were more likely to be living at home, unemployed.

If we go back to the high school years, we will find that the pendulum swings either far left or far right: parents are kicking kids out at age 18 or never. Gender Issues published a 2010 study conducted by psychologist Judy Kleinfeld. In it, she reveals there is a higher risk of suicide, conduct disorders, emotional disturbance, premature death and juvenile delinquency, lower grades, test scores and college attendance rates as compared to their female counterparts.

I attribute this sad state of affairs to the great divide. We have become a society of professionals and researchers who look to answer questions using new-fangled terms, new tests, and semi-longitudinal studies as proof that we've found the answers. There has never been a return to what worked. We say we don't want to reinvent the wheel, but that is what we do when it comes to human research. We tend to go for intervention as we attempt to save our youth. But organizations are seeking to genderize too many approaches. Boys and Girls Club, Boy Scouts, Girl Scouts, PACE Center for Girls, and others.

The programs that we offer, the antidotes that we offer, and the protections that we offer are geared toward just the girls, or just the boys, or just this race or that race, or just this age or that.

Yes, I am the first to recognize there is a rightful place for all of these programs. There is also a proven need for them, but not at the expense of what I will call the student body.

When I designed a program and later implemented it for the multicultural population at a local state college, the location and ambiance, our workshops and guest speakers attracted everyone.

In other words, programming was tailored to meet the previously unmet needs of various minority groups; however, we designed it in a way that met the holistic student developmental needs of all. Our award-winning program was designed by assessing the needs of our students first. My team applied best practices that would bolster our efforts and fit our program design.

If you were to ask me what I see missing in the secondary school system now, a number of words would come to mind, but the word Accountability is number one. Number two is Reality. Many of our students cannot distinguish between what's real and what's conjured (in a video game, for example).

The two previous words belong to the students. There are many that belong to the parent, but many of my students do not have the luxury of parental involvement or even parental concern.

So we will move on to the school's staff. There are many with different titles, a few of which I will list here: Dean of Conduct, Vice Principal of Instruction, Vice Principal of Scheduling and Data, Campus Advisor, School Resource Officer, Guidance Counselor, Teacher.

The following scenario should help you to get a general picture of a day in the life of a high school student:

6:45 a.m. – Student walks on campus and sits on a bench just feet from the entrance to the main office.

6:50 a.m. VP's begin to arrive or enter and exit the building (student is on his cell phone staring at the screen with ear plugs engaged).

7 a.m. Teachers begin to arrive or enter and exit the building (student is joined by another student who does not speak, but sits at the other end of the bench and commences to staring at her cellular device with ear plugs engaged).

More students, more teachers and a few Spanish-speaking parents arrive. There is constant movement. All students sitting and standing outside the buildings now are all on their cell phones, staring downward as if in another world.

Hearing nothing of the world that is high school. No interaction, no good-mornings, no "You are not in uniform", nothing. There is no place on campus that students "shouldn't be". The teacher who has reported seeing students making hot-and-bothered conversation in a parked car during lunch has commented that this occurs on a regular basis. Yet, she has not reported it, as she feels it is administration's responsibility to patrol the fringes of the school grounds and notice these things for themselves.

The adults on campus have expressed care and concern for the students. I have personally witnessed this care and concern. The students, however, have a different perception. "Nobody cares about us, Ms." "You're the only one who cares about us." I understand precisely what these students mean when they say this. But I can't tell them they are wrong, that others do care, because I know what caring means to them.

As Deion put it, it means not embarrassing a kid (even if it might appear that she deserves to be embarrassed) by calling her out in front of the class. "Dr. Carter, you pull us out into the hall and talk to us. You straighten us out in private."

We have to hold students accountable in every way. We can't become gentle and accommodating and forgiving when a consequence is in order. Denise is proof of that. She was an end-of-March newcomer. The email said she and her family had just survived a tragic loss. On the first day, she expected to be able to put her head down and wait out the bell. After all, it was 4th period and lunch was next. It is possible that in her first three classes, she was allowed to relax. That is not what she is here for. This is not a shelter. It is an education facility. A safe haven to learn and grow, not become academically stagnant and shrivel. She was resistant. Argumentative even. At first.

"I just got here."

"Yes, that's right, so you have a lot of catching up to do."

Since my students know me, they know that I expect us to help each other. They also know that I am fair in my distribution of expectations. This young lady's transfer grade was a high B. I don't care where a kid is coming from; when I see a B or A, I assume the kid is a hard worker and is willing to continue to maintain that record. The next day, she came in ready to work, but she somehow fell into a funk. Head down, she tuned out. I addressed her by name, instructed her on the work at hand, and walked away as she began to object.
"You have until the end of the period."

By the end of the semester, Denise finished the course with an A. Between the first day and the last, there were moments of teacher and student disagreeing, teacher handing student a poorly written essay, student refusing to take it, and teacher disposing of it in the trash. She got the picture. And there is no doubt in her mind that I care very *much about her life, her happiness, her safety, and her success.*

Then there is the student who is not so vociferous. Jake was isolated. He was not vocal. If I had to guess, I would assume he had experienced trauma that has gone unaddressed. No one, not his guidance counselor, not our behavior specialist, not even an ESE consultation teacher or 504 program coordinator has gotten through to him. He is un-approached. I see him alone all the time. Sometimes my eyes track his steps until he is out of sight, hoping to see him approach a friend. No such luck. After the south Florida school shooting, our school's student body decided to take an active role in protesting and speaking out against school violence. However, one of mine commented about Jake while Jake was in the room. "He'll probably be the one to shoot up our school, Ms." I knew he was wrong. Wrong for making such a statement about another person. But more wrong for pinning an uncommitted crime on a kid his own age. Yes, we know it happens. We know it has happened far too many times on far too many American school campuses. And even if Jake believed this kid was right about him, I needed to prove to both of them that he was wrong. So I addressed it within earshot of Jake.

One wheel we don't need to reinvent is providing them with role models. They are looking for someone they can emulate. If not at home, then at school.

When we really care for our students—male and female

alike—we show them tough love (according to Isaiah) and prepare them to launch.

Running on Empty

That's what happens when passion is all you have to keep you going because your leadership leaves you with a sense of alienation or uncaring and no support. Consider Mr. Hennessey, a 20-year veteran educator whose salary never exceeded 50 thousand dollars. Twenty years in the Florida Education system and he's leaving because he makes more money shopping for other people's groceries. True story.

June 19

We as a society have made a grave mistake as we attempt to do what's best for our children. We have taken terms and applied them to what teachers were doing all along before there ever were terms. There was a time many, many years ago when we didn't talk about evidence-based learning or data-driven decisions. We had good teachers who just looked at the information presented before them, interacted with the student, observed the student in his learning environment, looked at what the student could learn, how the student learned best, looked at how best to teach the material to the student, looked at all the facts, made her own notes and records, put all those pieces together and created a whole that would influence academic success.

At some point researchers decided we needed to call it something: "It's what's working, so let's call it something. Let's call it scaffolding; let's call it differentiated instruction; let's call it the Danielson method; let's call it Universal Design Learning. And then after we call it something, let's tell teachers this is how you should do your job." No one has ever, ever, ever gone to a teacher and said tell me how you teach and then I'll know what to call it, or let me watch you and see how you teach and I'll know what to call it. Rather, the teacher is asked to become familiar with a concept and prove its applications.

What came first, the chicken or the egg? What came first, effective instruction or terminology? I guarantee you effective instruction came first, because kids came first. And because we've allowed some poor teachers to slip through and stand in front of our students, we decided that all teachers must be required to go through the same rigorous training despite the fact that many of our teachers can actually deliver that training and add their own spin to it based on their experience, expertise, impact and success.

Let's compare professions and see what is required not only to enter the profession, but also to continue in it.

Eligibility to Teach

Educators are often asked, "Do you have to go to college to teach?" It is to laugh. I pulled some interesting facts from the Internet in order to add credence to my assumption that teachers are required to do more than other professions to be eligible to enter (and remain in) the profession.

Occupation	Starting Salary	Average Salary
Teacher	**38,712** (mycascades chools.org)	**45,723**
At least a bachelors degree	Completion of an approved teacher training program and possess a state issued educator certificate.	New, out-of-state or returning teachers must take FTC exams: Professional, Subject-area, and General Knowledge. Certification must be renewed every 5 school fiscal years and must include 6 semester hours of college credit and additional hours of in-service points.

Police Officer	36,340	57,160
Age 19 H.S. Diploma or GED	6 months of training Automatic bump in salary after academy	Seasoned officers with a break in service are exempt from Full-Recruit training
Fire Fighter	29,210	50,780
Age 18 H.S. Diploma or GED	3-6 months EMT-Basic certification Firefighter II certification Firefighter Minimum Standards Certified training	Out of state firefighters must take an Equivalency certification exam

Firefighters who are not actively involved in the fire service over the three-year period of certification are required to complete the Firefighter Minimum Standards Practical Renewal Examination.

Per the FDLE:

Someone who has previously served at least one year full-time in the past eight years as a sworn officer in another state, for the federal government, or for the military may qualify to be exempt from completing the Basic Recruit Training Program pursuant to s. 943.131, F.S.

Some might argue that teachers are charged with the young lives of other people's kids, so the stakes are higher. Stakes + Employ Me = Pay Me Accordingly.

Ours is a country of divided opinions as to the best way to go about educating our youth, thereby preparing the next generation of leaders. Those in position to make change (federal, state and district-level personnel) don't always agree with those who directly influence the change we seek (teachers). I hope I have alerted people to the fact that public school is not what we remember, and we need a well-crafted approach to reaching students if they are to ever launch out on their own (without a court order).

We are competing with technology in startling ways, and today's learner is more in-tune with what is happening in the surreal world of cellular devices and laptop screens than they are with humans with whom they come in contact every day. I hope this starts a dialog that includes a re-examination of the decisions made based on the dollar (and failed programming) so we can couple ample funding with education that is the catalyst for "Lift Off."

As the evening wanes, it occurs to me that this is really over. The school year is really over. Nothing else to journal about. So here are my final words.

As I stated in my introduction, I started journaling as a means of venting and reflecting. By nature, I am solutions-oriented. Once I express my frustration with a thing, I must determine a course of action to resolve, improve or eliminate whatever it is that's making life or learning difficult for me, or someone I know. I wrote this for anyone interested in the future of our children. I wrote this for teachers, and those who are not and have never been teachers, and I wrote this for all stakeholders who feel a sense of responsibility for our youth, for the next generation of leaders. I challenge each of us to balance evidence and data with experience and encounters.

Learned individuals with access to research will tell you that evidence-based teaching and data-driven decision-making is the way to go. I concur, to an extent. I was that teacher who was plunged head first into a classroom managed by an unseasoned permanent substitute who cared deeply for the students, but who admittedly "grandmothered" them to the point of complacency. I had no ready access to data or evidence beyond graded work their grandmother filed away for them in a drawer in the classroom. Decades ago, before I was ever able to tout experience or expertise, an Orange County Schools administrator advised me to rely on instinct and use common sense in this field. I generated my own data sets based on final grades from the previous quarter, work I scanned as I perused the folders, and my encounters with the students. I distinguished the extremely-bright-yet-rebellious from the extremely-bright-yet-under-challenged, the academically struggling from the easily distracted, the extremely-bright-yet-linguistically challenged from the student with disabilities. What I found missing from the equation was true discourse. I attended more than 30 meetings/trainings. Of those, two (2) involved true engagement of the professionals in the room, sharing best practices and anecdotes. In the determined effort to create a uniform system of effective teaching, legislators and trustees, principals and assistant principals have spoken to a handful of educators and decided what works. In a classroom with abilities and personalities as unpredictable as the severity of the next Florida hurricane, no training should begin without knowledge of the expertise in the audience, or end without a window of opportunity for shared insights.

Dr. Carter Makes a Few Recommendations
(12 to be exact)

1. A Specific Number of Training/Workshop/Seminar/Book Talk Opportunities should be offered at the beginning of the school year. Others can be added as the year progresses, but to start off, teachers should be given the opportunity to select which session they will attend based on the program description. Teachers should be required to have attended a maximum number, tracking their attendance, learning garnered, and a detailed discussion of how the learning was applied. These requirements are already part of the DPP process. The difference is in the numbers. All teachers should not be required to attend all the same sessions. Categories could be created to guide decision-making: Mandatory, Optional, Supplemental-Mandatory. Of the say, 20, workshops, 10 are mandatory, 5 are Supplemental-Mandatory, and 5 are Optional. In the course of a year, a teacher might be required to have completed a total of 5 sessions, three of which must derive from the Mandatory

category. The other two sessions can be selected from any of the categories, thereby satisfying a teacher's 5 required professional development-training sessions. If presenters or session designers anticipate low teacher turnout for what they deem an important topic, these sessions can be presented to the entire faculty during an in-service or other on-site activity sponsored by the school's principal.

2. Licensed Mental Health Counselors/Guidance Counselors

The student-to-counselor ratio is 250:1 or 900:1 depending on the school. 250 is recommended. The national average is 491:1. California and Arizona are in dire straits. In the good ol' days, counselors could speak to children for a few minutes in the office and send them on their way. They still do this, but how many students do they miss? You should know what a day in the life of a guidance counselor looks like. I'll pick Schedule Day. Teachers are given a schedule. On the designated day, we take our students to the media center where four (4) guidance counselors are set up. Throughout the period, each counselor calls the name of a student who approaches the table, takes a seat, and hands over the registration form they filled out for the coming year's classes. I don't remember how many days this went on, but I do know the bell rang before they could reach all the students who were present. Of course, a few were absent. That's another hurdle. Imagine what it's like when they meet with graduating seniors. No need to discuss how a day in the media center effects instruction. Rather, it is critical to understand the role of a guidance counselor is far more than scheduling or completing a Graduation Checkdown. Students who have no peer interaction need the opportunity to sit still in a safe and quiet place to discuss academics, goals, dreams and setbacks, even if for a few moments. I recommend increasing the number of guidance counselors, adding more licensed mental health counselors, and reducing the rising number of School Resource Officers. According to a March 2018 report (Sun Sentinel), our district will be granted an additional 100 million dollars to source the officers. An SRO can address violence in schools. A LMHC can address and often mitigate the triggers of violence. At PACE Center for Girls, Inc., a Florida-based, nationally recognized fleet of schools, licensed therapists and social workers are on-site the duration of a student's school day. I doubt there will ever, ever be an SRO presence there.

3. DPPs of Learning Cycles

This recommendation ties into the 12-12-17 entry. Student data should be pulled to reflect lowest performing and highest performing students. Administrators should make side-by-side comparisons of the teacher-produced DPP and student assessment data to analyze teacher approaches to student-centered instruction. Gaps should become apparent and those teachers with high performance ratings should be paired with teachers with low performance ratings to coach them toward success. Ideally, this should be done with teachers sharing similar populations.

4. Failure as a Sign of Success

Let Sebastia be an example to us all. She received ample redirection, attention, encouragement, reminders, warnings, prompting, private conversations, small talk, you name it. Still, she did what she had always done before my arrival. Stall. Bide her time. Goof off. She was counting on relationship to save her. We had a good relationship. We talked, we laughed, I involved her and called on her. But I could tell there was a pattern of coaxing teachers to accept late work, late as in one week before the end of the school year. I knew that she had established relationships with her ESE coordinator and guidance counselor. I knew that she had watched them advocate for her throughout the year. She counted on this same pattern to save her now. This will be just the lesson that leads her to success in the future if the powers that be don't cushion the life lesson with Brain Drain or some other easy out. I want her to be successful, but she must embrace the reality that time is of the essence.

5. Using the Jan 21 entry (last self-reflection excerpt) as an example:

Zari feared failure and assumed a Ph.D. would not be willing to help her or know how to help her. I started by listening to her in conversations with her peers. I saw her confidence when she spoke with authority. I saw her peers listen respectfully to her and often take her advice. I listened to her use words she could not spell. I heard her speak sentences she could never write correctly.

But in her spoken words, I heard her intelligence. Her grammar and sentence structure, her English skills, her composition skills needed to catch up. If we use what they produce as our primary or sole indicator of their abilities, we do them a disservice and create more work for ourselves. Take such a student aside and let her know what you see. This is data-driven instruction with a twist. Explain to her how you will use her strengths to eliminate her weakness. Finally, make it clear that you can only do it with her cooperation. As she so patently stated: Don't try? Never learn.

6. Post-training surveys

Surveys should be revised to eliminate the presumption that everything presented in a workshop is new and will be used for the first time after said workshop. Too often, I hear too many teachers express their disdain with a seminar or workshop that they could have led themselves. The survey questions are suggestive at best.

7. Funding

There seems to always be a shortage in some area of public education when it comes to ESE services, technology in the classroom, teacher aides and teacher-selected professional development. The flip side of that is the abundance of software options for course planning. The platforms and companies promoting them were endless, offering a plethora of ways to interact with students online, quiz students, track progress and plan lessons. Unless these platforms were bought in bulk, I wonder what the cost benefit is or if this was a grab at an opportunity to spend grant dollars. Otherwise, we need a true re-examination of the funnels through which all educational dollars flow. If there is excess, it should go toward teacher salary increases. One teacher shared, "I left this school system 13 years ago and was paid more then, than I am now." One district in my state is hoping for Board approval of more than 50,000 dollars to establish an early monitoring system in order to catch elementary school students who are academically at risk. Thankfully, I am not alone when I say this would be a waste of money. We have trained individuals who are with these kids face-to-face every day. They input the grades; you can't get an earlier warning system than that. The problem is with the curriculum. As I understand it, teacher-designed modules have replaced textbooks. All any teacher needs can be found in the A-Beka Curriculum and Dr. Seuss. Not the Dr. Seuss spin-offs. I am not a fan of those. A-Beka and Seuss.

8. Time…

As a former higher education administrator, I understand the Catch 22 involved when input is sought from all levels. It can chomp away at the limited time available to plan, execute and assess an initiative. However, without buy-in, or at the very least, input, from teachers, morale will quickly reach an all-time low. Teachers will not feel appreciated. They will not feel heard. They will only put forth a shell of a best effort for employment's sake. Too many good teachers exercise the transfer option, the retirement option (Like Mr. Hennessey, our professional grocery store shopper) or the just-enough option. Teachers are better than that. Since meetings are usually the time that input is sought and entertained, it is also the place where time is never adequate. Teachers should be given the option to submit written or recorded input. Written input should have a word-count limit. Videos, of course, would allow for more to be said, still with a limit (perhaps 2 minutes). Teachers should have group meetings to ensure concerns or suggestions are not duplicated. Surveys work, but they are all written and questions are guided. Biweekly meetings are designed to serve this purpose, but the only persons privy to the feedback are the administrators. Two meetings per year (one per quarter) should be devoted to sharing the top 2 or 3 ideas/concerns and the administration's plans to address them.

9. And Time

Thankfully, most teachers entered the profession, not for the summers off (many work a second job to supplement income), but to make a positive difference in the lives of students. An inordinate number of items are placed on a teacher's to-do list. They tend to make this discovery when they arrive in the morning and check their mailboxes. Upon reaching the classroom, there may or may not be an email further explaining the package taken from the box. "Teachers, please check your boxes for XYZ. This needs to be discussed in first period after disseminating blah blah blah." Or teachers could be asked to sketch out time for other important matters. Important, yes. But it takes precedence over instruction. "Discuss with students this and that. Send any students who (fill in the blank) to the media center. At the sound of the fire alarm, please wait for further instructions before evacuating." Time is critical, but it is on life support in the classroom.

In faculty/staff meetings, it would go a long way to thank teachers for accommodating these disruptions. Make a statement about the administrators' attempts to minimize disruptions, about how people who are sent to interrupt a class are trained in classroom etiquette so as not to call too much attention to themselves upon entry. Currently, too many messengers exercise zero protocol. Students need every minute of intstruction they can get.

And Time Again

I just wanted to briefly touch on a method I use in my classroom. I have two cell phones. I use one to keep time. I let students know what we have planned for the day and that we'll be using a timer to help us stay on task. Once I give them an assignment, I also let them know how much time they have to complete it before we move on to the next item. Using a timer helps the teacher and the student to monitor time, make good use of time, and, over time, it reduces the angst that usually accompanies the use of a stop watch. If I see a student getting off task, I simply say, "Focus" to redirect him.

10. Danielson

Danielson's methods have taken a slight beating throughout the book. New teachers tend to embrace it, as they should. They are in the learning phase of the profession, and many aren't sure what effectiveness in teaching looks like (notwithstanding memories of a favorite teacher). I recommend having a conversation with teachers to find out, specifically, what flaws they see in this approach to excellence. Some say they voted for a different framework. Others struggle with its applicability in the existing environment. As I mentioned earlier, if you have teachers who lived and breathed the method before it was given a name, they will be hard-pressed to go in reverse and attempt to match what they have already known to what has since been discovered. Metaphorically speaking, a baby engages in the act of walking before becoming familiar with the term. So to ask baby to prove knowledge of walking by check off motor development, cruising, locomotion and obstacle navigation is counterproductive.

11. When Kids Say the Darndest Things, Be Ready (From the Jan 26 entry).
Here are the eight statements with my responses and commentary.

1. <u>Can't we just finish it at home?</u> If you answer yes, it could mean no work during class time and incomplete work when submitted the next day. Instead, set the standard and stick to it. "You can finish anything at home that I see you working on all period in class. Otherwise, don't even ask me that. You know better."

2. <u>Can I go to the bathroom?</u> If you answer yes, it could mean a disappearing student who often returns with a snack from the vending machine. Instead, my response is always, "Let me see what you've done so far." No matter the objection, they know I am as serious as a full bladder. If we've been working for 20 minutes and a student can't produce work, I am unable to offer a pass to relief. They know now.

3. <u>You expect us to write 500 Words in 40 minutes?</u> If you answer no, it could mean you are granting them two days to take their time. Teach time management and the importance of making every moment count. Effort is more important than excellence. "At least 500. You're losing time asking me about the word count."

4. <u>Why didn't you grade my paper?</u> If you get this question from a student who did not head his paper properly (name, date, assignment, etc.), you might explain what it takes to record work. "Teachers must record work under a certain category with a corresponding date and weight. A headless paper makes that task impossible. Heading your paper

teaches responsibility, attention to detail and record keeping. When you get your graded work back, in my class or any other class, you know exactly what the assignment was and when you completed it. If there is ever an issue or question, you have evidence of your efforts."

5. Let go of my phone. Don't touch my phone. "One of us needs to let go of your phone. I will not fight you over a phone or anything else that you are obviously valuing over your own academic success. If it means that much to you, then you and your phone can leave. Tell me where you have to be right now, that your phone is that important?"

6. If I don't pass, I'll just go to Brain Drain. If you go to BD, you will not learn what you are supposed to be learning. BD is for you to have a second chance. That means you must take advantage of your first chance.

7. I'll copy someone else's [notes]. "You are alive; you are well. You have the capability of either pecking on a keyboard or grabbing hold of a pen or pencil using your fine motor skills, so you will write this while you have time."

8. I gave it to you; you lost it. "I have been known to lose money, but two things I don't lose are children and papers." Wean students off the need to cast blame on the teacher by drawing such a conclusion. "Okay, let's backtrack so we can figure this out together, because either way, I can't input a grade without the work."

Bonus: I almost forgot about this guy. He was transferred to my class after allegedly telling a teacher, "I'll f*ck you up." The worst he'd ever done in my class was demand that special pencil (see "Kids say the darndest things"). On this day, he levied his contractual rights against my request that he start working. "I didn't sign your little syllabus so I don't have to do your work." With a student like this, you smile as big is he smiles and say, "Once you entered my room, you accepted responsibility for your own learning. You have possession of my syllabus, so you are now liable for your own success in here. Sorry if you were misinformed." Then walk away.

Teacher of the Year

How does one garner such an accolade? Teacher of the Year is quite an honor, one that has never been bestowed upon me. Several other types of teaching awards, yes, but not teacher of the year. I don't personally know any recipients either. And that's over a couple of decades of friendships, camaraderie's and co-trainings. But I can talk to you about a Teacher of the Year who was recently in the news. She is a very influential teacher who does what I have seen many teachers do. She labeled her students and predicted their futures. One child in particular in her kindergarten class would go home and tell his mom what a bad kid he was. He reported that he'd heard that from his teacher. He didn't say the teacher told him that. He took on that description and believed the teacher, thereby internalizing her perception. If this were a case of the child's word vs. the teacher's, I would have presented it to you differently. No. The teacher was caught on tape saying these things to the child. She spoke negatively of the mother as well.

USAToday, Foxnews and CBSnews each reported on this story. A teacher working in the Miami Dade County School district used the word loser to describe the boy on several occasions and told little Aaron his mother was driving her crazy. "Aaron, y tu losers." She said she didn't like Aaron's behavior. Huh?

"You still don't know how to write? I don't know what to say to your mom. She is driving me crazy. Why is she driving me crazy?
"I feel sorry for your mom. I really do. She is a little lost."

"Raise your hand if you know how to bubble. Aaron doesn't know. He's circling."
Maybe she just needs more teaching experience in order to understand why this behavior is counterproductive, damaging, unprofessional, unethical (and a litany of other adjectives). That's not it. She is a 32-year veteran. Thirty-two years. Plus the

recipient of the 2017 Teacher of the Year award from her school. And no one would have suspected this. Not in a classroom full of five- and six-year-olds. I added this story to make my final recommendation.

12. Avoid lackadaisical evaluations for the seasoned and often decorated professional. I would venture to guess teachers with enough experiential years either don't get evaluated or receive 5-minute visits and a pat on the back. 32-year-old roofs, 32-year-old cars, 32-year-old anything else, would get a thorough examination to make sure everything is still functioning properly and up to code or standard, that is, if they are not sent to the junk heap.

Mrs. Rosalba Suarez might well have a leaky roof, or be in need of a timing belt, or an unannounced classroom visit that lasts the entire period. Otherwise, we run the risk of an abuse of power (remember my November entry?).

Sadly, she is not alone. This seems like an isolated incident, but I doubt she is the first to abuse her power at the expense of young minds and fragile souls. How can we be sure this isn't happening elsewhere, and if it is, how can we put a stop to it?

Some colleges utilize the peer evaluation method. Rather than have administrators meet unreasonable deadlines due to limited manpower, trained teachers can pay their colleagues a visit (announced and unannounced). Better still, retired teachers can volunteer to take on some of this responsibility. Of course, trained administrators would still conduct the summative evaluations. Those with as much seasoning salt on their resumes as this Ms. Suarez should be required to share something new they adopted into their professional practice. If not new, then a technique or strategy they hadn't used in some time, how it benefitted the students and a bit of reflection on how it impacted planning, instruction, outcomes, collaboration, assessment, student comprehension, engagement, or some other aspect of the teaching and learning process.

Enough said.

I didn't share everything that happened. No time for that. I wanted you to get the picture. I hope you got the picture. You got a bit of my perspective, my expertise and my attitude. I have a great deal of respect for so many people in this field. I watched some shed tears over kids, over rules, over red tape, over feelings of being undervalued. I have enjoyed many days of laughter with these professionals. And I have seen teachers offer support like few in other professions. The sacrifices are beyond your imagination. The risks they take are daily reminders that they don't do it for the money. What money? My starting salary was in no way commensurate with my years of experience or my three degrees. Summers off are spent working a second job for many of them. Still others join administrators who greet students after they've been patted down, marched through metal detectors and inspected for weapons. I haven't forgotten about you. Those stories take the trenches and horrors to another level.

Teachers may never be compensated their worth, but if funds were directed in places and ways that would lighten the load a bit – computer labs (not just carts), licensed mental health counselors, an increased number of guidance counselors, stipends for proficient teachers to help the basic performers and for distinguished teachers to take in-service days to give demonstrations or collaborate and take over classrooms for a day, that would do wonders for teacher morale and starkly reduce the teacher turnover rate even in the worst performing schools. Imagine what the future would hold for the snot-nosed kid who is destined to be tomorrow's leader.

I love you guys. Stay positive and stay strong. For the children.

References

[1] "Predator" teacher gets 22 years for sex with students. July 3, 2015.CBS News.

[2] Kelman, Brett. Fifteen kids reported this pedophile. They left him in the classroom anyway. March 22, 2017. The Desert Sun.

[3] Sex addict teacher asks to spank female colleague. January 31, 2018. https://www.youtube.com/watch?v= BNbNj4jV9w

[4] Police: Oklahoma teacher found drunk, pants- less at school. Aug 11, 2014. ABC News.Wjla.com

A Beka. Pensacola Christian College. abeka.com

Adolph, K.E. & Robinson, S.R. (2011). The road to walking: What learning to walk tells us about development. In P. Zelazo (Ed.) Oxford handbook of developmental psychology, NY: Oxford University Press.

Firetactics.com/blog. How long does it take to become a firefighter? Retrieved 2018

Florida teacher quits ob to become full-time shopper. July 8, 2018. News Channel 8 WFLA. Guidance counselors are underfunded. 2016.The Atlantic.com

Kleinfeld, Judy. 2010. The state of American boyhood. *Gender Issues.*

Kozol, Jonathan. 2005.The Human Cost of An Illiterate Society.

PACE Fast Facts 2016. PACEcenter.org

Schools may not be able to add enough school resource officers. March 27, 2018. Sun-Sentinel.com

Silverstein, Jason. July 6, 2018. Mom secretly records son's kindergarten teacher calling him a loser. CBSnews.com

Exhibit

High School English Department
English III
Course syllabus January – June 2018

Teacher: *Dr. P. Carter*
Email: *pCarter@sian.edu/k12*

Course description: In this course, we will study American literature as found in non-fiction, fiction, poetry, drama and oratory. Focus will be given to textual evidence as used in student writing, research, discussions and presentations. The study and application of vocabulary and grammar will take place within the context of what is read and written during the course.

Please note: Additional supplemental texts, activities and assessments will be selected based on students' needs. Core standards/Measurement Topics: By the end of the course students will be able to do the following: **Reading:** Read, comprehend, analyze and evaluate complex literary and informational text independently and proficiently
Analyze points of view and cultural experiences drawing on a wide reading of various genres of literature
Writing: produce clear, well-supported and coherent writing (argumentative, narrative and informational, as well as process) routinely over extended and shorter time frames in which the development, organization and style are appropriate to task, purpose and audience.
Conduct short as well as more sustained research projects synthesizing multiple sources to answer a question or solve a problem
Speaking and listening prepare for and participate effectively in a range of conversations and collaborations including the presentation of information and supporting evidence in which organization development and style are appropriate to task purpose and audience
Evaluate a speaker's point of view, reasoning, use of evidence and rhetoric
Language: Demonstrate independence in gathering vocabulary knowledge when considering a word or phrase important to comprehension or expression
Demonstrate command of the conventions of standard written English, grammar, usage, punctuation and capitalization

textbooks Ball of Light collections

Grading policy Course grades are a reflection of the student's level of academic achievement in regards to the content standards. A student's 9 weeks grades will be computed as follows:

-Diagnostic assessments 0%

-Formative assessments 40% (average of assignments and assessments)

-Summative assessments 60% (average of assignments and assessments)

Students and parents can access course grades on APEX located on the Cascade County website HTTP://www.mycascadeschools.org under CIMS (Cascade instructional Management System) located in the toolbox/resources of the parents tab. You will need your child's account information provided by the counseling department.

Retakes students are allowed at least one retake for 1 summative per quarter. There are no retakes for formative grades. Retakes for summatives must occur before the next semester summative assessment is given.

Classroom Expectations

Cellular devices:

Phones must be put away (out of sight) before entering the classroom.

Tardy Bell: Begin working on sweet tweets before the tardy bell rings.

Bathroom breaks: Bathroom breaks will not occur on a daily basis for the same students.

Spare time: If you complete your work early you are not permitted to put your head down. You are not permitted to use your cell phone. You must pick up a book or Magazine from the bookshelf or bring a book from the Cascade High School library (a pre-approved alternative is also acceptable)

Sleeping: Sleeping is never acceptable or permitted. If you are found with your head down you will be asked to sit up and re-engage in the learning. If it seems difficult for you to do so, you will be asked to go and wash your face to help you wake up. If you are hesitant or refuse to go get refreshed, you will be sent on referral to the front office.

Working with other students: If you are assigned a partnership and you refuse to get with a partner, you will be awarded half credit for the assignment that you turn in (Example: if the quality of the work submitted is equal to a 90, you will be assigned a 45 in the Scorecard). Certain aspects of team work are being measured when partnership and group work is assigned. These collaborative skills cannot be assessed if you work alone. If you are assigned to work in a group and you choose to work alone you will be assigned a fraction equal to **1/3** or **25%** of the grade.

If you work in a group and do all the work, yet willingly divide the credit for that work, each member, including you, will be penalized in the Scorecard (Example: you list 3 individuals on your PowerPoint presentation and two of them did not contribute. The quality of the work is equal to a 100. The grade assigned will be a **33** for each member.)

If you are working with a partner or in a group on the first day and are absent on the day the assignment or presentation is due, you will receive half credit for the assignment. However, you will be permitted the opportunity to make up the other half by completing an individual presentation. These individual presentations are given standing at the lectern in front of the class, not seated at your desk.

Dr. Carter will conduct **Random Checks**-- random folder checks and random note checks. Please refer to the rubric for the grading scale of notes and folders as well as self-reflection essays and other assignments.

Formative assessments are precursors to the **Summative**. In other words, formative assignments are equally as important as summatives, so it would behoove you (it is incumbent upon you) to treat formatives as seriously as you would a summative. Remember, the smaller assignments prepare you for the larger assignments.

Please refrain from asking if this is for a grade. Every assignment and activity must be placed in your folder, which will ultimately become your portfolio. Your portfolio must be presented at the end of the grading period in the order outlined in your syllabus.
*I strongly recommend you purchase a 3-prong, 2-pocket folder (15 cents at Walmart) to begin building your portfolio.

Assignments:
Some assignments must be completed in class and submitted during class; therefore, you are required to use that time wisely and make every effort to complete assigned work when time is allotted for completing work in class. This work is not to be placed in your folder or backpack and taken with you. You must show significant progress in class before asking Dr. Carter for permission to continue working outside of class.

*Assignments must be headed properly with your name, the due date, your period and the title of the assignment.

Assignments graded as a collaboration need only be placed in 1 student's folder. All of the group members will be assigned credit for possession of that assignment when portfolios are graded.

Attendance:
Attendance is weighed heavily in this course, as each day and each assignment and activity is a link to a very large chain.
Preparation and Participation: Coming to class prepared means arriving with a pencil and/or pen, at least 2 sheets of paper, and any homework that is due.
Homework: Homework will range from an assignment, to study material, to completing a task: read a short story, gather research, clip a newspaper article, get a form signed by your parent/guardian or something else. You are expected—I repeat— you are expected to come to class prepared. Homework is critical to certain projects we will undertake in this class, so please establish a strategy for remembering to complete or prepare your homework.
Absences
We will adhere to the School's attendance policy. For each day of absence you will be awarded that same number of days to make up missed work. All missed work is located throughout the room. All activities are recapped on the bulletin board (See Recap). Your classmates are also a resource, as am I. Please utilize the resources available to you so that we can make sure you stay on track. Please keep in mind, however, that you are ultimately responsible for work missed.
Communication and Protocol
In an English classroom, communication takes many forms. Please make use of all opportunities for communication by first raising your hand if you have a question during class; by approaching my desk with permission; summoning me to your desk by raising your hand; jotting down a brief, polite and appropriate note regarding any academic issues, concerns or questions you might have; emailing me; seeing me during lunch; or scheduling after school time.
Questions about Scorecard
Please check Scorecard on a regular basis no fewer than once a week. If in the event you find that a grade is missing or there is some other discrepancy with your grades, please bring that to my attention at the appropriate time: at the end of class, via email, during lunch or simply jot me a polite note. Include your name,

period, and specific concern. I check grade concerns within a few hours, as I know how important your grades are to you.

Classroom disruption: Disruptions can take many forms such as arriving late to class and calling attention to yourself. If you are late and are unsure of whether or not I've taken attendance, please approach my desk to make your presence known to me. A simple, "Dr. Carter, I'm here" is sufficient.

Respect:

-Personal space is defined as space within one foot of another student's desk.

-Kind words are the only words we should speak to one another in the classroom (and outside).

-Insults: Insults do nothing to enhance the learning experience or boost another person's self-esteem; therefore, it is not permitted.

-Profanity: You will be expected to conduct yourself with dignity in our classroom. This includes sidebar conversations that you think can only be heard by you and your neighbor. Profanity is not permitted.

-Name calling is not a term of endearment and therefore is not permitted.

-Cleanliness: disposal of trash is not a sport. Move quietly to the trash can and dispose of your garbage; do not try to "shoot it" in the can.

Eating: Full meals are not permitted in the classroom. You may produce a snack and eat it quietly disposing of your trash, but no sandwiches, plates, or baked goods are permitted. Set them aside when you enter. No excuses. If you intend to share with large numbers of classmates, you will be permitted to do so during the last minutes of class time.

Plagiarism: Make sure you do your own work at all times. If you use sources to complete assignments, you must give credit to your source(s) by citing the source(s) within the text and at the end of your work on a Works Cited or References page.

Dress code: CHS has established a uniform and dress code policy. Please make sure you wear clothing that fits you. This means under garments are not to be exposed at any time.

-END-

Subscribe to Dr. Carter's mailing list:

askdrpoochie@gmail.com

To schedule workshops or training, contact us:

INFO@3one7media.com

www.ingramcontent.com/pod-product-compliance
Lightning Source LLC
Chambersburg PA
CBHW051955090426
42741CB00003B/1404